Map of North Kerry

Locations shown on the hand-drawn map:

- BEAL
- LETTER
- CARIG IS.
- CARRIGAFOYLE
- LECK
- ASDEE
- AHALANG
- TARBERT
- TARMON
- DOON
- POCKEENEE
- BALLYBUNION
- GLANALAPPA
- EGGANANE
- BROWNS
- CRATOO
- BALLYNOE
- CASTLESHANNON
- BALLYMACHDAM
- LISTOWEL C.
- BALLINRUDDERY
- LIXNAW
- ABBEFEALE
- ARDFERT
- LISCAHANE
- BALLYBEGAN
- CRULEE
- CASTLEISLAND
- RATASS
- BALLYCARTHY
- CARRIGNAFEELE
- BALLYMULLEN
- BALLYMACELLIGOT
- BALLYBELGH
- ARABELLA
- DRUM
- CLONMELANE
- MOLAHIFF
- CASTLEMAINE
- KILCUSHLAN
- KILMURRAY
- ARDNAGRATH
- CASTLEMAINE
- FIERIES
- BALLYPUMOTH
- KILORGLIN

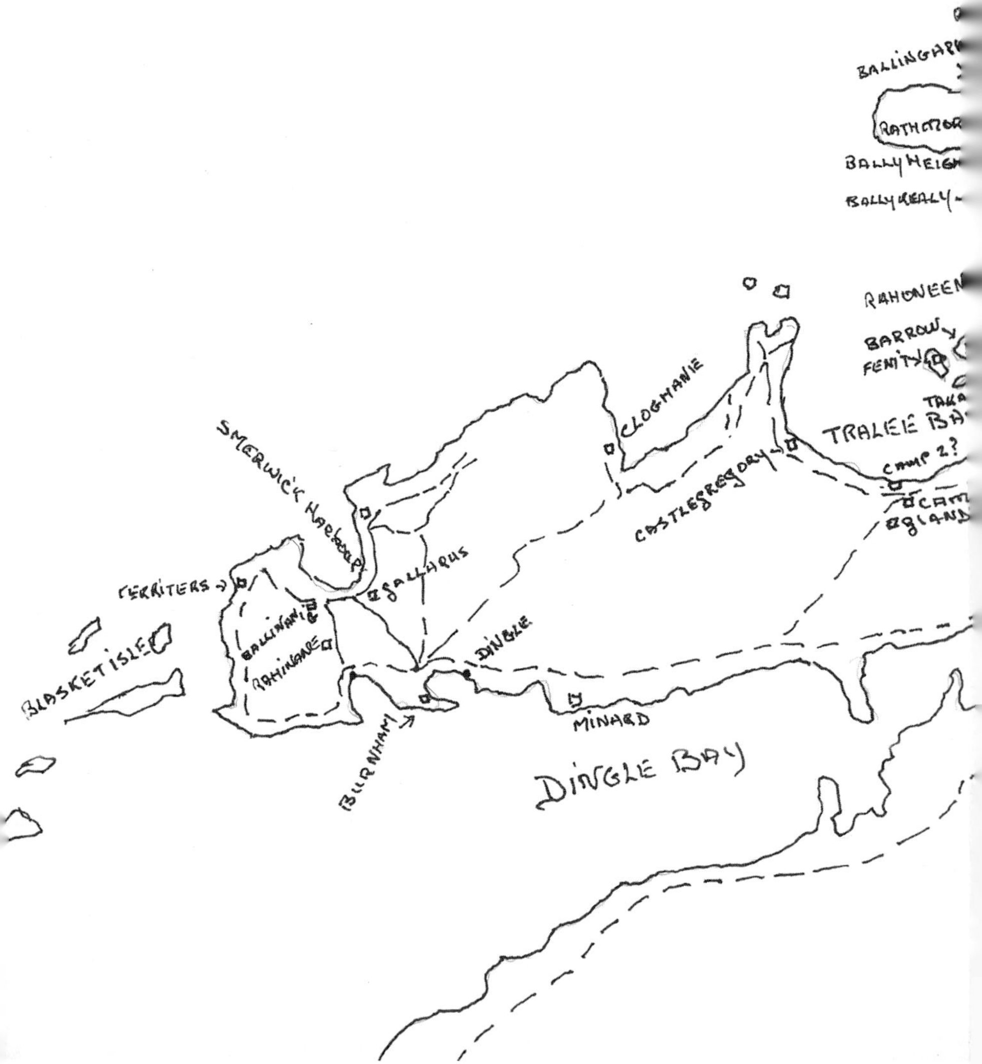
BARROW
FENIT
CLOGHANE
CASTLEGREGORY
CAMP 2?
SMERWICK HARBOUR
GALLARUS
FERRITERS
RAHINANE
BLASKET ISLE
DINGLE
MINARD
BURNHAM
DINGLE BAY

The Geraldines

Thomas Davis

The Geraldines! the Geraldines!—'tis full a thousand years
Since, 'mid the Tuscan vineyards, bright flashed their battle-spears;
When Capet seized the crown of France, their iron shields were known,
And their sabre dint struck terror on the banks of the Garonne;
Across the downs of Hastings they spurred hard by William's side,
And the grey sands of Palestine with Moslem blood they dyed;
But never then, nor thence till now, have falsehood or disgrace
Been seen to soil Fitzgerald's plume, or mantle in his face.

The Geraldines! the Geraldines!—'tis true, in Strongbow's van,
By lawless force, as conquerors, their Irish reign began;
And, O! through many a dark campaign they proved their prowess stern,
In Leinster's plains, and Munster's vales, on king, and chief, and kerne:
But noble was the cheer within the halls so rudely won,
And generous was the steel-gloved baud that had such slaughter done!
How gay their laugh! how proud their mien! you'd ask no heralds sign—
Among a thousand you had known the princely Geraldine.

These Geraldines! these Geraldines!—not long our air they breathed,
Not long they fed on venison, in Irish water seethed,
Not often had their children been by Irish mothers nursed,
When from their full and genial hearts an Irish feeling burst!
The English monarchs strove in vain, by law, and force, and bribe,

To win from Irish thoughts and ways this "more than Irish" tribe;
For still they clung to fosterage, to *breitheamh*, cloak, and bard:
What king dare say to Geraldine, "Your Irish wife discard?"

Ye Geraldines! ye Geraldines! how royally ye reigned
O'er Desmond broad and rich Kildare, and English arts disdained:
Your sword made knights, your banner waved, free was your bugle call
By Gleann's* green slopes, and Daingean's tide,† from Bearbha's∫ bands to Eochaill.§
What gorgeous shrines, what *breitheamh*∆ lore, what minstrel feasts there were
In and around Magh Nuadhaid's¶ keep, and palace-filled Adare!
But not for rite or feast ye stayed when friend or kin were pressed;
And foemen fled when "Crom abú"** bespoke your lance in rest.

* Angl. Glyn   † Angl. Dingle   ∫ Angl. Barrow
§ Angl. Youghal   ∆ Angl. Brehon   ¶ Angl. Maynooth
** Formerly the war cry of the Geraldines, and now their motto.

Ye Geraldines! ye Geraldines! since Silken Thomas flung
King Henry's sword on council board, the English thanes among,
Ye never ceased to battle brave against the English sway,
Though axe and brand and treachery your proudest cut away.
Of Desmond's blood through woman's veins passed on the exhausted tide;
His title lives—a Sassanach churl usurps the lion's hide:
And though Kildare tower haughtily, there's ruin at the root,
Else why, since Edward fell to earch, had such a tree no fruit?

True Geraldines! brave Geraldines! as torrents mould the earth,
You channelled deep old Ireland's heart by constancy and worth:
When Ginckle leaguered Limerick, the Irish soldiers gazed
To see if in the setting sun dead Desmond's banner blazed!
And still it is the peasants' hope upon the Cuirreach's* mere,
"They live who'll see ten thousand men with good Lord Edward here."
So let them dream till brighter days, when, not by Edward's shade,
But by some leader true as he, their lines shall be arrayed!

* Angl. Curragh

These Geraldines! these Geraldines! rain wears away the rock,
And time may wear away the tribe that stood the battle's shock,
But ever, sure, while one is left of all that honoured race,
In front of Ireland's chivalry is that Fitzgerald's place;
And though the last were dead and gone, how many a field and town,
From Thomas Court to Abbeyfeile, would cherish their renown!
And men will say of valour's rise, or ancient power's decline,
"'Twill never soar, it never shone, as did the Geraldine."

The Geraldines! the Geraldines! and are there any fears
Within the sons of conquerors for full a thousand years?
Can treason spring from out a soil bedewed with martyr's blood?
Or has that grown a purling brook which long rushed down a flood?
By Desmond swept with sword and fire, by clan and keep laid low,
By Silken Thomas and his kin, by sainted Edward! No!
The forms of centuries rise up, and in the Irish line
COMMAND THEIR SONS TO TAKE THE POST THAT FITS THE GERALDINES!

The Castles of the Kingdom

Michael J Carroll

ACKNOWLEDGEMENTS

This book is dedicated to the Clans of Kerry and their descendants

I wish to thank all those who assisted me in my research, compiling notes, typing, and the preparation in getting this book to print. Special thanks to Dick Richards for assisting in research, Redbarn Publishing for proofreading, editing and typesetting the final draft for printing, Upper Case in Cork for preparing the illustrations, and GraphyCems (Spain) for printing.
The cover as well as all the black-and-white illustrations are by Alan Langford of Southampton.
A special thanks to John Pierce of Listowel and Eamonn Brown of the Kerry County Library whose assistance is greatly appreciated.

Text © 2004 Michael J Carroll

Published by Bantry Studio Publications, Bantry, Co. Cork, Ireland

First published in 2004

First issued as a Bantry Studio Publication paperback 2004

All rights reserved. No part of this publication may be reproduced, stored in a retrieval system or transmitted in any form or by any means, electronic, mechanical, photocopying, recording or otherwise, without prior permission of Bantry Studio Publication.

This book is sold subject to the conditions that it shall not, by way of trade or otherwise, be lent, re-sold, hired out or otherwise circulated without the publisher's prior consent in any form of binding or cover other than that in which it is published and without a similar condition including this condition being imposed on a subsequent purchase.

British Library Cataloguing in Publication Date
Michael John Carroll
The Castles of the Kingdom
Ireland: Local History. Irish History

ISBN: 0 9519415 5 0

Illustrations by Alan Langford
Printed in Spain by GraphyCems

Contents

Preface	1
Introduction	5
Aghadoe Castle	41
Ahalana Castle	44
Arabella Castle	44
Ardea Castle	45
Ardfert Castle	47
Ardnagragh Castle	48
Ardtully Castle	49
Astee Castle	50
Ballinanig Castle	51
Ballinskellig Castle	52
Ballingarry Castle	53
Ballinruddery Castle	54
Ballybeggan Castle	55
Ballybunion Castle	56
Ballycarbery Castle	59
Ballycarnaghan Castle	61
Ballycarty Castle	62
Ballycushlane Castle	62

Ballygrellagh Castle	65
Ballyheigue Castle	66
Ballykealy Castle	67
Ballymacadam Castle	68
Ballymacaquim Castle	69
Ballymalis Castle	72
Ballymullen Castle	74
Ballynoe Castle	75
Ballyplimmoth Castle	76
Barrow Castle	77
Beal Castle	78
Bebhion Castle	80
Brewsterfield Castle	82
Brown's Castle	82
Burnham Castle	83
Caher Castle	85
Callownafersy Castle	85
Camp Castle	86
Cappanacushy Castle	86
Carrigafoyle Castle	88
Carriganass Castle	92
Carrignafeela Castle	95
Castlecore Castle	97
Castle Cove Castle	100
Castle Craig	101
Castledermot	101
Castle Gregory	102
Castleisland Castle	104
Castlelough	105
Castle MacEllistrim	107
Castlemaine Castle	108
Castle Quin	112

Castle Shannon	113
Cloghane Castle	113
Clonmellane Castle	114
Currans Castle	115
Derryquin Castle	115
Dingle Castle	116
Doon Castle	120
Drum Castle	121
Dunamark Castle	122
Dunboy Castle	123
Dunkerron Castle	125
Dunloe Castle	129
Dursey Castle	132
Fenit Castle	134
Ferriter's Castle	135
Fermoyle Castle	138
Fieries Castle	139
Gallerus Castle	141
Glanalappa Castle	145
Glandine Castle	146
Kilcushnan Castle	146
Killaha Castle	147
Killorglin Castle	148
Liscahane Castle	150
Listowel Castle	151
Letter Castle	154
Litter Castle	154
Lixnaw Castle	155
Minegahane Castle	157
Minard Castle	158
Molahiffe Castle	160
Moorstown Castle	162

Palice Castle	163
Pookeenee Castle	164
Punt Castle	165
Rahinane Castle	166
Rahoneen Castle	168
Ratass Castle	170
Rathmorrel Castle	171
Rattoo Castle	171
Reenavanig Castle	172
Ross Castle	173
Short Castle: No. 1	178
Short Castle: No. 2	179
Short Castle: No. 3	179
Tallagh Castle	180
Tarbert Castle	181
Tarmon Castle	182
Tralee	182
Tralee Castle	183
Trant Castle	186
Appendix I (List of Alternate Names)	188
Bibliography	189

Preface

Following the success of *The Castles and Fortified Houses of West Cork*, which has been reprinted a number of times, I was asked to document the castles of Kerry in something of a similar style. If I had been aware of the difficulties that I would encounter in researching this book, I would not have commenced the work.

Knowing the history of West Cork and almost every square mile of the region, I found little difficulty in writing the history of the castles, as I had visited the majority of these edifices during my earlier research into the history of West Cork.

A very high percentage of the castles of Kerry have been obliterated from the landscape. In fact, both King and Colman at the turn of the last century only list about seventy-eight castles in the present county, which was roughly half the number found in West Cork. When I first enumerated all the castle names that I sourced I arrived at over a hundred and fifty. This was mainly due to the fact that many castles were known by different names depending on who was in occupation at a certain period of time (See Appendix page 188). In fact, one castle had seven different names. Furthermore, a number of castles in different locations were known by the same name, which added to the confusion. For instance, there were four Short Castles in Kerry.

Most of the castles listed in this work have fairly comprehensive histories in their own right, while others have disappeared from the landscape and their exact location is unknown. Even local history and folklore have little or nothing to add, as they are only listed in passing so that they will not be forgotten. Maybe, just maybe, somebody some day will find some old document which will throw light on the history of one of these forgotten castles.

The remains of the castles, fortified houses and tower houses are the vestiges of a bygone era where the Anglo-Normans and clan leaders lived in relative safety.

Each has its own story to tell, whether it is family history, siege, fire, attack or bombardment by cannon fire. When visiting the ruins one can almost hear the closing of heavy doors, feet running up the spiral stairway, shouting and laughter in the chambers, and the strains of music coming from the great hall, or the cries of battle, the clash of swords, screams of the injured and the echoes of cannon fire. The advent of gunpowder and cannons changed the nature of warfare in Ireland. Castles were no longer impregnable structures when under concentrated fire.

There were many long sieges, when fire and battering rams were used to gain access while boiling oil, stones, arrows and spears rained down from the battlements. Walls were eventually breached or weak corners caused the castles to collapse. When access was finally gained, the slaughter of those inside was often savage and on most occasions no one was spared. Even the women, children and servants were put to the sword.

Now with cattle and sheep sheltering in the ruins of the

lower cellars, and blackbirds, crows, pigeons and jackdaws making their homes in the upper ivy-covered walls, we are inclined to forget the past, until a strange indistinguishable sound is heard and it is as if the ghosts of the dead are signalling that someone is encroaching on their domain.

This book is designed to whet the appetite of those interested in local Irish history and to tempt the visitor to take a few steps back into the turbulent years of Kerry's past. In addition to historical facts, some of the castles have their own legends and tales of ghosts still walking the battlements. These have been documented where possible.

Introduction

Castles are defined as fortified building of stone whether they be watchtowers, single tower houses or buildings with two or more towers which sometimes were referred to as fortified tower houses or mansions. They were principally built for defensive purposes. Some were just of two storeys while other had up to five storeys. Firstly built by the Anglo-Normans as a means to hold onto their conquered territory, the Irish tribal chiefs recognised their importance and followed the foreigner's example and abandoned their earthen forts with timber-framed accommodation in the centre which were very vulnerable to the fire-arrows of the Anglo-Normans. In time, the castles evolved into fortified residences for both the Anglo-Normans and the Irish chieftains. Like in West Cork the castles are nearly all of the basic design with the ground floors of the castles being defensive with access at the second floor level. All were rectangular buildings with one or more projecting angle towers for defensive purposes. Within the castles were small chambers, spiral stairways in a corner wall and the odd dungeon at ground level. The majority had barrel vaults over two floor levels, bartizans, running machicolations, and loops for either gun or crossbow.

Some of the major castles had bawns or outer enclosures which varied in size from forty six feet by twenty six feet to a hundred and sixty feet by eight feet. The bawns were usually guarded by projecting mural towers with gun loops as a first line of defence. Within some of the bawns were small out-houses, stables, storerooms and small gardens. When Henry IV in 1429 sanctioned a grant of £10.00 to his subjects and to those who had pledged allegiance to the Crown. This grant, in those days, which continued into Elizabeth's reign, was a substantial amount of money and this signalled the increase of castle building. Soon the tower houses were no longer adequate as family homes and the Anglo-Normans and the Irish clan leaders began to build fortified houses or mansions which were either joined to the existing tower house or stood alone nearby. Few of these remain today as revealed in the following pages.

In this short history of Kerry's years of castle building, it is not my intention to rewrite this particular phase of the Kingdom's history, which extended over five hundred years. Maybe some energetic young historian can undertake this work in the future. Availing of all the major sources, I have tried to hold the 'middle road' and to give an impartial account of what happened during the era in question.

To draw a contrast with what happened during the period AD 1200 to AD 1700, I have decided to commence with the Viking/Danish invasions, especially those involving Kerry and West Cork, when the clans and tribes forgot about their petty grievances and joined together to engage and defeat their common enemy over the course of some three hundred years of warfare, both on land and on sea. I have not included ecclesiastical history, as this would constitute a book in its own right.

After a period of time conquering the east and south coast of Ireland, where they made their settlements in Dublin, Wexford, Waterford and Cork, the Danes began to move down along the west coast. In AD 807 they ravaged Innishmurry off Sligo and plundered inland. Four years later, in 811, they ventured up the Shannon, made a base in Limerick and then attacked the monastery of Clonmacnoise and others. The following summer they moved further south and plundered the Skelligs and the monastery at Ballinskelligs. Returning the following year, they encountered the Eoghanacht tribes of west Munster and were defeated in a sea battle off the Kerry coast.

This reversal did not deter them and they returned with more ships and fighting men and set up their southern base on the Island of Dursey (Thor Iy) off the Beara peninsula. In 823, they moved further inland going up the Kenmare river and also to Bantry Bay, where they ravaged and pillaged every monastic settlement in their search for gold and silver and enslaved the young women.

Again in AD 869, the Irish clans of Ciarraighe, Uí Conaill and the Eoghanacht of Lough Lein came together and defeated the invaders, who lost many of their fighting men. This was repeated the following summer when they arrived with over a hundred ships and about four thousand hardened warriors. Being an obstinate and proud race, the Vikings did not give up easily. They engaged in battle with the Irish on the Kerry coast and were defeated with great losses on both sides.

When Magnus, son of Olanus, son of Arailt, King of Norway, was not satisfied with the homage of Morough O'Brien, the king of Ireland whose kingdom only extended over the central and eastern parts of Ireland, he assembled a large fleet from both Norway and Denmark and set sail with enough men to finally conquer Ireland *c.* 945. He was determined to take revenge and to kill all those who had obtained victories over his earlier kinsmen and allies.

After encountering a severe gale his fleet was dispersed. He, with his wife, his principal leaders and some two hundred of his best fighting men eventually landed on the coast of Ireland. Before the main fleet of ships arrived, the Irish, under the leadership of Morough O'Brien, attacked the camp of the Norwegians and after a fierce battle killed the king, his wife and all his retinue and fighting men. When the main fleet arrived a few days later and learned of the death of their king and his wife, they returned north with the bodies of the dead to give them a proper Viking burial in their own homeland.

Aware of the victories of the southern clans over the Norsemen, Brian Buru travelled south to meet the clan leaders at Kealkil outside Bantry and seek their assistance before the impending battle at Clontarf, where many of the Kerry chieftains were killed, including the O'Connors, Scanlans, O'Donoghues, O'Mahonys, Duggans, O'Moriartys, O'Cahills, Harringtons, O'Sheas, Donegans and over ten thousand southern fighting men (refer to G. Keating).

During the next hundred years, the clans of Cashel and the O'Briens made many incursions into south Munster knowing that the forces of the indigenous clans were utterly depleted after fighting against the Vikings. This period of Munster history is poorly documented. All we know is that they raided as far as Killarney, Tralee and the northern part of the Dingle peninsula, pushing the local tribes further south to the edges of the sea. Amongst those to be displaced were the O'Moriartys, O'Cahills, the O'Falveys who held the Dingle peninsula, the O'Sheas who held Iveragh, the O'Congaile who held the western part of Magunihy, and the O'Donegans and the O'Lynchigh, who held most of the Beara peninsula.

Introduction

The MacCarthy clan came onto the scene when Turlough Mór O'Connor, King of Connaught, set up an Eoghanacht chief as a rival to the O'Briens. His name was Tadgh, son of Muireadhach, son of Carthagh. Dividing Munster into two kingdoms, he set up Tadgh as King of South Munster. Anxious to annex as much territory as possible, Cormac MacCarthy swiftly moved down into Kerry and banished the O'Moriartys, O'Conors of Ciaraighe and the O'Sheas of Corca Duibne. These in turn sought help from Turlough O'Connor, whom they had assisted in many wars and been loyal to in the past.

During the following year, the Moriartys and the O'Sheas arrived back in Corca Duibne and the west of Kerry with ships and a sizeable force and regained most of their territory and even went up the Luane river with boats to engage the MacCarthys in battle. Cormac was deposed by O'Connor in 1127 and ended up in Lismore Abbey, but he was later reinstated by the O'Briens. With the second banishment of the Kerry clans, a period of clan warfare continued, with the O'Briens assisting the local chieftains. Battles, raids, burning and killing continued.

The MacCarthy army invaded the areas around Loch Lein, Iveragh and most of the southern part of Desmond, but was eventually met by O'Connor Kerry and most of the Kerry chieftains, who drove back the incursion of the MacCarthys. Realising that he was losing, MacCarthy entreated O'Connor of Connaught to assist him.

From this we see how fickle the existing situation was in Ireland—how the various kings or leaders changed from one side to the other when they saw a possible advantage to further their own gains—and at the decisive battle of Moin Mhor in 1151, the local tribes were defeated and the MacCarthys strengthened their position in north Kerry and Desmond.

Tadgh was succeeded by his brother Cormac, who incidentally was responsible for the building of Cormac's chapel on the Rock of Cashel. Another Turlough, the son of Rory O'Connor, succeeded to the throne of Ireland in 1130. He was followed by Roderick, his son. In 1138, Cormac MacCarthy was murdered in his own castle on the Rock. His sons succeeded him in turn. Some time later, in line of succession, Donal Mór O'Brien got possession of north Munster while Dermod MacCarthy ruled south Munster. This temporarily ended the rivalry and warfare between the two clans.

The O'Donoghues followed the MacCarthys south at about this time, c. 1140, and initially moved into County Cork, where they encountered the O'Mahonys, O'Driscolls and other local clans. Following a number of battles, especially one at Ballincollig, the O'Donoghues moved almost completely into Kerry and displaced the clans of the O'Carrolls and O'Cahills, who were in possession of the lands around Killarney. It is reputed that one of the O'Donoghues, Amhlaoibh Mór O'Donoghue, built the church at Aghadoe c. 1158. He was later killed in battle. During the following years, the other chieftains of the O'Donoghues didn't have much luck. At least three of them were assassinated or killed by either the O'Moriartys or the O'Cinneade during the following twenty years. During this time, with the Anglo-Normans at their doorstep, the inter-clan warfare continued with the O'Donoghues evicting the O'Connells out of Magunihy. The O'Donoghues were now in full control of their new territory and paid tribute to the MacCarthys; they moved into Beara and Kenmare and accepted the MacCarthys as their overlords. They had abandoned their ancient home and territory along the Suir river after being forced out by Donal Mór O'Brien and the advance of the Anglo-Normans from the east.

Introduction

Before the intrusion of the MacCarthys, the area known as Corca Duibne was ruled by the O'Falveys and the O'Sheas and these were later joined by the O'Cuilein (O'Collins), who had forsaken their ancestral lands in north Limerick. They defended their territory strongly until the arrival of the Anglo-Normans by sea on their coastline, where they erected fortifications and castles. Suffering attacks from both the Anglo-Normans and the MacCarthys, they were gradually overrun and became nothing but serfs to their conquerors.

*

Digressing, momentarily, to the arrival of the Anglo-Normans in Ireland, the whole situation changed in Ireland during the reign of Roderick O'Connor, when the wife of Teigernan O'Rourke left him and sought refuge with Diarmuid MacMurrogh, King of Leinster. O'Rourke went to Roderick requesting help to recover his wife. Roderick, upset by his ally's predicament, raised a great army and marched into Leinster and defeated Diarmuid MacMurrogh, who was force to flee the country leaving his consort safe in a monastery. Arriving in France, he sought help from Henry II, King of England, to regain his kingdom. With authority from the King to raise troops, Diarmuid crossed back to England and then on to Wales where he met Ralph Griffin, the Viceroy of Wales, who put him in touch with a number of knights. These were Robert Fitzstephens and his cousins Maurice Fitzgerald and De Carraun (Carew), who the Viceroy wanted out of the country, as they had been spreading sedition against the King. Diarmuid and the knights came to an agreement whereby they would raise some troops and come over to Ireland the following summer. Having promised his daughter Aoife and the town of Wexford to Fitzstephens, Diarmuid returned to Ireland incognito and sought refuge in a monastery.

With the arrival of Fitzstephens and the other knights and a small force of three hundred footmen near Wexford, Diarmuid, with some five hundred horse soldiers, went to join them. He granted the town of Wexford to Fitzstephens and gave a tract of land to another knight called Hermon Morty, an emissary of Strongbow. Finding now that he had a force of over three thousand, Diarmuid swept into the territory of Ossory, where he obtained the submission of Donough, the King of Leinster. Alarmed at what was happening, Roderick O'Connor, the King of Ireland, raised a large army and marched towards Ossory to engage Diarmuid in battle, but he was forced to retreat with his army into the woods and forests. Eventually peace was arranged whereby Diarmuid would get back his kingship and territory and the Anglo-Normans would depart the country. The second part of this agreement was never fulfilled.

Fitzgerald arrived in Wexford the following summer with a small force. Diarmuid marched with his army to join him. The peace was now truly broken.

With the combined forces of the Anglo-Normans and his own army, Diarmuid marched to Dublin and the city surrendered. However, his ambitions went further, he wanted to become King of Ireland like some of his ancestors but he awaited the arrival of Maurice Fitzgerald with more men and supplies before he embarked on further conflict against Roderick O'Connor. Meanwhile, the Earl of Strangwell sent over Redmond de la Grose and William Fitzgerald to appraise the situation in Ireland. They immediately set up a fortification near Wexford and successfully defeated an attack by the King of the Decies (Waterford) with much slaughter.

The following day, St Bartholomew's Day, the Earl of Strangwell (Strongbow) arrived near Wexford with over two hundred knights in armour, a thousand bowmen and many foot soldiers. He was immediately joined by Diarmuid and the other Anglo-Normans and the combined force marched on to Waterford, which they captured with much bloodshed and slaughter. The army then marched to Dublin. Diarmuid thought it was time he had vengeance for the murder of his father, who was buried with a dog by the people of that city. While the inhabitants were negotiating a peaceful surrender, Miles de Cogan and de la Grose attacked the city from the north side and, having breached the walls, carried out a slaughter of every inhabitant they encountered, including women and children.

Having secured the city, Diarmuid and Strangwell marched on Breifne and laid waste the countryside leaving nobody alive. Roderick O'Connor, on learning of these atrocities, tried to make peace knowing that the opposite force was now greater and more powerful than any army he could muster.

On learning of the successes of the Earl of Strangwell in Ireland, Henry II of England, fearing that the Earl might declare himself King of Ireland, immediately issued a proclamation forbidding all shipping, correspondence and trade with Ireland under pain of death. Even though the Earl sent messages to the King assuring him of his total loyalty, Henry made immediate plans to go to Ireland himself. He landed in Waterford in 1172 with a large force of horse and foot soldiers.

When news of his arrival filtered through Ireland, all the Anglo-Normans arrived to pay homage. Diarmuid MacCarthy Mór of South Munster was the first Irish king to come and swear fealty to Henry II and submit to his authority. He even gave one of his sons as a hostage. This pledge of allegiance to a foreign king was the downfall of the great clans of Munster and brought about an almost immediate incursion of the Anglo-Normans into the domains of the reigning clan leaders.

At Cashel, Daniel O'Brien, King of Limerick and Thomond, also submitted to Henry II. Realising the advantages of the submission of the various Irish kings, Henry immediately sent sections of his army, under his trusted knights, to occupy both Cork and Limerick, while he himself advanced on Dublin where he received a warm welcome.

Roderick O'Connor, King of Connaught and Ireland, had little option but to do likewise. Happy to have gained the submission of all the kings of Ireland without a battle, Henry returned to England, but not before he had installed his trusted knights in authority over all the major cities and towns. This was the beginning of the domination of the Anglo-Normans in Ireland which lasted for over eight hundred years. In this day and age, we probably could compare Ireland in the twelfth century to Yugoslavia in this century, but with a common religion and culture.

*

Diarmuid MacCarthy was happy for the following few years in Munster, until Henry granted most of Cork and Kerry to Fitzstephens and Miles de Cogan, his trusted knights, for services rendered to the Crown. With the Anglo-Normans beginning to make inroads into his kingdom, Diarmuid tried to make peace and granted a tract of land in the Lee valley to Fitzstephen and de Cogan.

Diarmuid was murdered in his own castle by Theobald Walters, a member of the house of Ormond, in 1185. He was succeeded by his son, Donnell, who was a highly impetuous young man. Gathering his forces, he drove the Anglo-Normans out of Limerick, took possession of the city and recommenced hostilities against the O'Briens, who began to gain what territory they could in Thomond.

From 1195, with the Anglo-Normans on their doorstep, the inter-clan warfare continued and within a few years the

O'Donoghues had driven the O'Connells out of Magunihy. They were now in full control of their new territory under the MacCarthy Mórs. About this time, the O'Sullivans moved into Beara and the Kenmare area and accepted MacCarthy as their overlord. They had abandoned their ancient home and territory around the Suir river after being forced out by Donal Mór O'Brien and the advancing Anglo-Normans from the east.

Before the intrusion of the MacCarthys, the area known as Corca Duibne was ruled by the O'Falveys and the O'Sheas, and these were later joined by the O'Cuilein (O'Collins), who had been forced to move south. They defended their territory well until the arrival of the Anglo-Normans by sea on their coast and the advance of the MacCarthys. They were gradually overrun and became nothing more than serfs.

In 1194, Donal Mór O'Brien died and, during the struggle for his succession, the Anglo-Normans seized the opportunity of gaining more territory, while the Eoghanacht tribes advanced as far as Limerick, which they held for a short period.

In 1197–8 Hamo de Volgnes, the chief justice of the Crown, granted tracts of land in east Limerick and north Kerry to the sons of Maurice Fitzgerald. When John became King of England in 1199, he granted Meiler Fitzhenry the barony of Uí Ferba (Tralee to Brandon). In 1200, the O'Briens and the Anglo-Normans invaded Cork county and parts of Desmond. From this particular year the real invasion of Kerry commenced. In that same year, the Anglo-Normans started raiding north Kerry and came as far as Killarney as the O'Donoghues struggled to hold on to their newly gained territory.

Donal Mór MacCarthy died in 1206 and a struggle started between Dermod and Cormac Fionn as to succession, with the Irish and Anglo-Normans on both sides.

While this struggle continued, the Anglo-Normans under Meiler invaded from Limerick. When Geoffrey de Marisco became justiciar, he married the widow of Thomas Fitzgerald's brother and became guardian of young Maurice Fitzgerald. He was now in possession of most of the Dingle peninsula and as far as Dunloe.

Thomas's two sons, John and Maurice, together with their cousin Thomas Fitzrobert, strove to gain more land and, with the assistance of Thomas Fitzanthony, carried on the conquest of north Kerry beyond the Maine river.

Meanwhile de Cogan and Fitzstephens, already holding most of the coastline of West Cork, moved into Kenmare Bay and built more fortifications. Thus, with castles along the Maine on the north and the line of fortifications along the Roughty river, the kingdom of Desmond was shrinking by the year, while O'Connor Kerry still managed to hold on to a small section of his territory in north Kerry.

Geoffrey de Marisco's son inherited the lands on the western half of the Dingle peninsula, Castleisland and Killorglin castles and lands. All of these lands were confiscated in 1234 when Geoffrey killed the Earl Marshall and his son was accused of trying to kill the King.

After the turn of the thirteenth century, Desmond stretched from north-east Cork to the west coast of Kerry and was ruled by the MacCarthy Mór. In Kerry, there were the O'Donoghues and the O'Sullivan Mór who accepted the MacCarthys as their overlords, while in Kenmare and the Beara peninsula, O'Sullivan Mór and O'Sullivan Bere did likewise. North of Desmond in Kerry were the O'Connor Kerrys, situated between the O'Briens of Thomond and the MacCarthys, as if occupying the buffer zone in a brief time of relative peace. But now, with a new MacCarthy leader about to appear, everything was about to change drastically.

During this period of conquest, the Anglo-Normans—having gained possession of the cities of Cork and Limerick, including most of the present counties of Wexford, Waterford, Tipperary and Limerick—began to move further south into north Kerry and south Cork. They began to build castles of stone and mortar along the coastlines of both counties to consolidate their hold on any territory gained. Seeing the advantage of these strongholds, the Irish chieftains followed suit and built their own castles as a means of protection and to hold on to their dwindling lands.

In 1214, Finghin MacCarthy's successor, Dermod Cluasach, fought a battle against the combined forces of the O'Briens and the Anglo-Normans and put them to flight. But, as happened with most Irish clans at that time, a quarrel commenced with his brother Cormac Fionn, who had fought against him with the O'Briens. While they went into conflict with each other, the Anglo-Normans pushed their advantage by building more castles and consolidating their hold on newly gained territory. Somehow, both brothers sorted out their differences and entered a pact with some of the Anglo-Normans and the local conquered tribes of Kerry against Hugo de Lacy and O'Neill, who were trying at that time to gain sovereignty over Desmond and had advanced as far as the Reeks and the lands around the estuaries in the following year (1215). In 1216, the rents and dues of Iveragh and elsewhere in his domain were paid to the head of the Geraldines at his castle at Killorglin. It should be mentioned at this point that Dermod MacCarthy had married into an Anglo-Norman family and taken a wife called Petronella de Bloet.

The other Normans kept pushing forward in conquest. Having seized all east Cork, Limerick and north Kerry, they advanced southwards towards the Reeks, while they came by sea along the Kerry coast. They continued building castles such as Dunkerron, Cappanacushy, Dunloe,

Castlemaine, Molahiff, Calanaferse, Cluain Maolain, Currans, Lixnaw and Castleisland.

In 1234, the MacCarthys under Dermod Fionn, founder of the MacCarthy Mór family, attacked Tralee Castle. He was killed with many others by John Fitzthomas, who held the castle. Meanwhile, Dermod's brother Donal Goth had established the house of MacCarthy Reagh in West Cork. A few years later he was murdered by John Fitzthomas and his son, aided and abetted by the O'Donoghues of Killarney.

Donal Goth was succeeded by his eldest son, Finghin, who had all the traits of a powerful leader. He gathered fighting men from all the MacCarthy septs and his father's allies, including the O'Mahonys, O'Donovans, O'Hurleys and O'Sullivans. He attacked the Norman castles along the coast of West Cork south of the Bandon river.

The following year, still full of anger after the murder of his father, he marched into Kerry as far as Killarney, where he attacked the O'Donoghues in their abode. O'Donoghue, his wife, sons and many of his Norman friends and servants were burnt to death in the conflagration. Satisfied that he had partially avenged his father, he led his army into north Kerry, plundering and burning the lands of the Anglo-Normans and driving them out of that part of the county. He returned home to West Cork and began to augment and train his forces for his next move. During the next two years he captured most of the Norman castles along the West Cork coast and banished the Anglo-Normans from his newly acquired territory.

The Anglo-Normans under John Fitzthomas agreed to confront Finghin. Having secured the assistance of Donal Gall (the foreigner), son of Cormac Fionn MacCarthy Mór, they marched out of north Kerry to confront Finghin. When word came to Finghin that this force was in Macroom and heading south, he retreated over the mountains from Bantry into Kerry by the Borlin valley. With his enemies in hot pursuit, he picked the most advantageous location to engage them in battle. This was a piece of wooded land between the Slaheny and the Ruachtach rivers where they joined. He waited, wondering if the enemy would enter his trap. By this time some of his best men were in armour and carried swords, lances and bows captured from the Normans.

Thinking that Finghin had only a few hundred men who could easily be defeated, John Fitzthomas Fitzgerald, together with his son and the son of Walter de Burgo, pressed forward. His force contained over a hundred knights in armour, some four hundred heavily armed foot-soldiers, bowmen, and the Irish allies under Donal MacCarthy of Desmond. They encountered a force of some hundred men on the rough terrain sloping to the valley beneath. Pressing their advantage, they entered the wood, but here the heavily armed knights on horseback were at a disadvantage.

There followed a complete rout as the Irish hiding in the heavy undergrowth picked them off easily. The knights were pulled from their horses with hooped polls and killed when they hit the ground. Estimates of the Norman losses range between three and five hundred men, including Fitzthomas Fitzgerald, his son, the young De Burgo and many knights. Finghin's losses were minimal.

The death of the leader of the Munster Geraldines and other noble knights presented a serious setback to the Anglo-Normans in Munster. The victory itself gave added impetus to the struggle. Now the Irish knew how to dictate their own type of battle against the Normans and their professional soldiers. Encouraged by the success, Finghin, having been joined by extra men, continued into Kerry and took Dunkerron, Cappanacushy, Ardtully, Ross, Glenflesk, Ballymalis, Killorglin, Molahiffe, Cluanmellane, Fieries, Castlemaine, Ballycarbery and Letter castles from the Anglo-Normans.

After this exhausting effort, Finghin and what remained of his own force returned to West Cork and journeyed to Kilbrittain. Anxious to drive out the Norman De Courceys from the Kinsale area, he laid siege to Ringrone Castle on the Bandon river. Miles de Cogan, who was in charge of the castle defences, sent messengers out to gather the existing Norman forces around Kinsale and it was agreed that both forces would attack the Irish besieging force at night. Taken by complete surprise, the Irish force was completely crushed in the mayhem of the sudden attack. Finghin and his trusted officers were all killed and the survivors fled. With the death of Finghin, the Irish resistance to the Anglo-Normans collapsed both in West Cork and Kerry.

After the death of Finghin MacCarthy Reagh, Donal Gall, who had fought on the side the Anglo-Normans, reaped the fruits of Finghin's victories and declared himself King of Desmond. He turned against his Anglo-Norman allies and drove them out of most of his territory. His son and his grandson, Cormac Mór, continued to fortify their possessions, which now stretched from the river Maine to the boundaries of Bantry. The Anglo-Normans began to regain most of their castles and lands outside of Desmond under Gilbert Fitzjohn and the Lord of Lixnaw, who both held them for the grandson of John Fitzthomas of Tralee Castle. When he came of age in 1282, he inherited most of the Geraldine properties which stretched from Waterford to Limerick and north Kerry. He was wise enough to keep peace with the MacCarthys. In 1296, he supported King Edward in the conquest of Scotland with a strong force of knights, bowmen and foot soldiers, but he died two years later, mortally wounded. He was succeeded by his second son called Maurice after his first son Thomas died unexpectedly. He became the first Earl of Desmond. During the following two decades, there was relative peace in Kerry with the Anglo-

Normans becoming more Irish than the Irish themselves, mainly due to inter-marriage. Edward I of England was not happy with the situation and began to impose taxes on imports and exports, especially from the main ports that Desmond was controlling—mainly Dingle and Tralee—as he had been informed by his aids that he was losing a great deal of revenue.

*

Despite its importance in south Munster in the struggle against the Anglo-Normans, the Battle of Callan received only a passing comment from earlier historians. It is now accepted that if Finghin MacCarthy had lived and continued to lead the Munster tribes, the Anglo-Normans could have been driven out of Munster before reinforcements could arrive from England.

It was a time when the Anglo-Normans were trying to consolidate their hold on south Munster, especially in the counties of Cork and Kerry, by building fortified stone castles along the coastline and on conquered territory. The Irish could not engage the Norman forces on open land, as the iron-clad horses and knights together with the armour-protected foot soldiers and archers operating in a well-organised battle formation, were impossible to defeat. Only the valour and bravery of the Irish, who were dressed in ordinary clothes and armed with pikes, swords, axes and spears, was feared by the Normans. At that time, the whole region was covered in forests, woods, bogs and rough terrain, so the Irish fought a running battle and then vanished into cover where they could not be followed. This tactic was hit-and-run and the beginning of guerrilla warfare.

In Kerry, the Normans advanced southwards. Using the city of Limerick as their base, the Geraldines, the most prominent of the Anglo-Norman families, built castles along the Shannon, along the coast and in north Kerry, with the precise objective of conquering Desmond, which was dominated by the MacCarthy clan.

Edward, the King of England, died in 1307 and was succeeded by Edward II, and three years later the third parliament in Ireland was held in Kilkenny, where the representatives of the Anglo-Irish nobles, clergy, and two representatives of each county, including Kerry, took part.

The years between 1315 and 1318 were years of instability in Ireland and began with the arrival of Edward Bruce from Scotland. Maurice Fitzgerald, the future earl, supported Edward II of England, while Diarmuid MacCarthy sided with Bruce.

In 1316, both the Fitzgeralds and the MacCarthys raided Corca Duibne, driving out the English freeholders. In 1325, Diarmuid MacCarthy was murdered in Tralee by William Fitzmaurice and other associates. William was blinded on the orders of Maurice and his accomplices were hanged. In the following years, Maurice strengthened his position and became like a petty king in Kerry.

During the regency rule of the Queen Mother, after Edward II was deposed, Maurice was created Earl of Desmond, but lost the title again when Edward III ascended the throne. However, he was reinstated in 1334 after spending two years in jail in Dublin. In 1339, the Lord of Kerry instigated an uprising in Desmond and was captured and starved to death in the dungeons of Castlemaine Castle. Maurice contacted the kings of France and Scotland and the Pope, inviting help, as he intended to become King of Ireland. In 1345, he marched to Kilkenny to seek the assistance of the other Anglo-Irish lords but he had no success and died in 1358 without fulfilling his ambitions.

He was succeeded by Gerald, known as Gearóid Iarla. He got involved in a struggle between the O'Briens and, having suffered a severe defeat, was captured by Brien O'Brien and had to be ransomed. During the following year, Cormac MacCarthy Mór died and was succeeded by Donal Óg.

When Richard II visited Kilkenny in 1390 he received the homage of the majority of the Irish princes, including O'Neill, O'Connor, O'Brien, MacCarthy and others.

At this time Tadgh MacCarthy accepted Gearóid of Desmond as his overlord, while he styled himself Tadgh MacCarthy Mór. A few years later, in 1398, Gearóid died in mysterious circumstances in his castle at Castleisland. His son soon followed him to the grave, having been mysteriously drowned in a nearby lake. His daughter Katherine had already been banished from her home after being discovered having an affair with her brother. She ended up in the care of the Earl of Ormond, who raped her. She poisoned the Earl's wife and took her place as head of the household.

In 1411, the sixth earl of Desmond was called Thomas. Aged about fourteen years, he was banished from his kingdom by his uncle James. He returned with an army in 1417 and ravaged Desmond and then assumed his earlship. He departed to France the following year and his uncle James succeeded him and consolidated the power and strength. This seventh earl did more for the Desmonds than any of his predecessors. He ruled over the east of Cork, controlled all the ports of Cork and Kerry and could rely on the help and assistance of the Knight of Kerry, the Knight of Glin, the White Knight, the Baron of Lixnaw and the O'Briens, while remaining on good terms with the Earl of Ormond. The Irish clans—the MacCarthys, O'Sullivans, O'Donoghues and the O'Donovans—paid him tribute. Not satisfied with his army of horsemen and kerns, he brought in the Scottish gallowglasses called the Sheehys. When he died, he was succeeded by his son Thomas, who was a personal and loyal friend of Edward IV. Amongst his most notable achievements was the setting up of a type of university at Youghal, which was based on the one at Oxford. Most of the male heirs from Munster attended this college, including Donal Cam O'Sullivan. In 1467, when he attended an enquiry in Drogheda, he was falsely found guilty of treason and beheaded. Angered by his death, his five sons gathered all the forces they could muster, including those of the MacCarthys and the O'Briens, and marched to Dublin where they ravaged and laid waste the Pale. The Munster Geraldines fell from power after this event and Desmond was ruled by the Kildare Geraldines until 1535.

From 1487 to the end of the century, the Desmonds were involved in various political escapades, as they refused to swear allegiance to the Crown. In 1487, James, the ninth earl, was murdered in Rathkeale by friends of his brother John.

He was succeeded by Maurice who put his brother John to death for his part in James's death. In 1491, Maurice sided with Warbeck, a pretender to the English Crown, and besieged Waterford. Lord Poynings came to the city's rescue and, with the first use of cannon in Ireland, dispersed the besieging force. Some time later, Maurice was pardoned by Henry VII.

Meanwhile, in Kerry, during all these escapades and involvement with English politics concerning the Crown and Ireland, the MacCarthys and the other clan leaders in Kerry and West Cork were content to enjoy life, except for the usual raids on adjoining territories. When not out hunting deer and wild boar, they were content to entertain each other in their castles, each trying to outdo the other in good food and entertainment, while on the side they showed off their mistresses.

The beginning of the sixteenth century saw the Irish, especially the Geraldines, seeking help from the Continent but without success. All that came were arms and munition. James, the eleventh earl of Desmond, signed a treaty with Francis I, King of France, in 1523, whereby Desmond was to supply four hundred horses and ten thousand fighting men to oust Henry of England, but this came to nothing. James of Desmond began an affair with a widow and his wife brought an action against him for conjugal rights. Her action succeeded and she returned to him.

The relative peace was shattered when the thirteenth earl of Desmond and O'Neill revolted in 1539. This became known in history as the Geraldine League rebellion. However, the revolt was unsuccessful when the promised help from the Continent did not arrive. Henry VIII, who was on the English throne at this time, demanded that those who had risen up should renounce the Pope and his influence in Ireland. Desmond, MacCarthy Mór, MacCarthy Reagh and O'Sullivan Bere complied. In 1542, Desmond and other chieftains were ordered to carry out a survey of all the monasteries and to dissolve them. However, little was done in this regard as far as Kerry and Desmond were concerned. In the same year, Henry VIII declared himself head of the Church in Ireland.

In 1558, Garret, the sixteenth earl of Desmond, succeeded as heir. He happened to be the son of his father's second wife. In fact, his father James had at least four wives, following the exploits of Henry VIII. He was a headstrong and impetuous man engaging in many petty rivalries, including one against his half-brother, Thomas Roe Fitzgerald, who had been disinherited by his father. In one affray, he was about to engage in battle with over five thousand men against the Earl of Ormond, his bitter enemy. Only for the arrival of his first wife, who happened to be a Butler, the two parties would have engaged in battle. His second wife, Elinor, would prove her strong character later in aiding him when he was imprisoned in London and when he was subsequently on the run. She proved herself a truly remarkable women, holding the house of Desmond together, and deserves a place in Irish history, like all the famous women who have gone before her.

Garret was placed under house-guard in London from 1562–4 and, despite his many misdemeanours, was even allowed to visit the royal palace where he often met Elizabeth, who was totally enthralled by his dashing good looks and sense of humour. The palace buzzed when he made his appearance and Elizabeth fell under his charm. When he succeeded in gaining his release from London, he joined up with MacCarthy Mór and O'Sullivan Bere and began to make forays into Ormond's territory to gather rents, and from this moment onwards all the Desmonds were in trouble. These conflicts now became a struggle for religious freedom.

Having made his peace with the Earl of Desmond, one of the latest adventurers called Stukely went to Spain and to the Pope on his behalf to seek assistance.

Fitzmaurice, meanwhile, retreated into the almost impenetrable woods of the Glen of Aherlow in Tipperary. There were many rumours of a Spanish fleet arriving at Dingle but Stukely was encountering great difficulties in getting foreign help.

Around this time, Ormond was permitted to leave London. He immediately marched south and arrived in Kerry, where he was aided by Fitzgerald, O'Sullivan Bere and the MacCarthys.

In 1571, a president and a council were set up to rule Munster. Also, a new country comprising south Kerry and a part of West Cork was created. This was to last until 1606.

The group of English adventurers, who had arrived in Cork, pursued their claims to be descendants of some of the early Anglo-Normans and immediately began to claim territory gained by their forefathers. One of these was Sir Peter Carew, who claimed all the lands from Dingle to Lismore in County Waterford and some of the Butler lands in Leinster. These false claims resulted in another Desmond rebellion and immediately a delegation was sent to Spain to seek the assistance of the Spanish king. With the arrival of a large shipload of arms and ammunition, the struggle commenced under the leadership of James Fitzmaurice, with the English, under Gilbert, commencing once again a 'torched earth' policy. This was eventually followed by a temporary peace.

Perott, with the aid of the MacCarthy Mór, took to the field in Kerry and laid siege to Castlemaine Castle for over five weeks, but, due to the lack of cannon and powder, the siege had to be abandoned. The siege recommenced the following summer and after about three months the garrison surrendered just before Fitzmaurice arrived to lift the siege. He was immediately pursued throughout Kerry and finally surrendered, near Aherlow, and the short rebellion was crushed. Fitzmaurice was pardoned but still kept in contact with Spain, hoping for assistance from the Spanish king. When he learned that his wife was writing love-letters to Edward Fitzbutler of Ormond, he quickly divorced her and married the widow of O'Connor Kerry and came into the possession of Carrigafoyle Castle, but was finally removed to London where he remained in gaol.

Queen Elizabeth released Desmond against the advice of her court in 1573 on condition that he would stay under house arrest in Dublin. By the end of that year, he fled Dublin and returned to his stronghold in Kerry, where he resumed his palatine rights as leader. By Christmas he was attacking Castlemaine Castle but was forced to hand it back the following September. Knowing that he could not hold on to his position without foreign help, he departed to France in 1573 and also travelled to Spain and Rome seeking military assistance.

Eventually, he got some thousand men from Pope Gregory XIII with arms and artillery. Stukely joined him and was put in charge of the expedition and sailed to Lisbon. Seeing that the king of Portugal was preparing to sail and attack Morocco, Stukely joined him with his ships and the expedition force hoping for a quick conquest and riches, but this was not to be. Both himself and the young king were killed and the depleted invasion force returned to Lisbon with losses of over half of the papal force.

Hearing of the disaster, Fitzmaurice departed from Spain and arrived in Dingle in July 1579 with money, a papal delegate and some eighty men. He immediately called for a Catholic revolt against the Crown and was quickly joined by his brothers, Sir John and Sir James Fitzmaurice. Seeking help in Connaught, James journeyed north but was killed by the Burkes of Castle Connell over a trade in horses.

The rebellion broke out in Connaught and Leinster but Fitzmaurice did not declare himself, knowing full well that he was not strong enough for a major revolt, even though many of the minor clans rose up. Lord Kerry, O'Connor Kerry and the O'Donoghues of Ross Castle joined the revolt but MacCarthy Mór kept his powder dry.

Sir William Pelham was in command of the Crown forces in Munster at this time. He was a shrewd and calculating leader and adversary. Knowing that Desmond was still a threat to peace, he first instigated the storming of all the castles and fortifications of the Desmonds, killing all the defenders, including women and children, as well as carrying out a 'scorched earth' policy to reduce the inhabitants that supported the Desmonds to famine conditions.

Thomas the Earl of Ormond returned from London and became Lord High Treasurer, President of Munster and

Lieutenant of the English forces in Ireland. He was known as An Thierana Dubh or the Black Lord. In March 1580, he marched with a sizeable force into Kerry and headed for Dingle, where he had been informed that Desmond had his arms and artillery. On the way, he ordered that everyone be killed including women, children, and all animals. Houses and crops were also burned. The devastation was recorded in local history as one of the greatest atrocities ever experienced in Kerry.

Finding nothing of a major threat, the English force then marched to Carrigafoyle and the almost impregnable castle was bombarded by cannon fire until the defending garrison surrendered. When the castle fell in late April 1580, everyone was put to the sword or hanged. These included Irish, Italians, Spaniards and the women and children. After this event, Pelham placed garrisons in those castles which still stood.

A few months later, Pelham and Ormond made a sudden raid into Kerry from Cork. Pelham marched to Castleisland while Ormond went to Glenflesk, after being joined by many of the Munster chieftains, including O'Donoghue Mór.

The two forces joined together and marched to Dingle where the English fleet under Admiral Winter had just arrived. What they found was a town in ruins and the castles fired by John of Desmond and the Knight of Kerry. Earlier, the Earl of Desmond and his wife had just escaped from Castleisland before Pelham arrived. Not prepared to give up the search for the Earl of Desmond, Ormond went into MacCarthy territory and burnt everything, including the crops as far as Cahirciveen. Finally, giving up the search, the combined armies headed back to Cork.

Up to August that same year, the Earl of Desmond remained on the run. He slept rough in the woods with a few servants and bodyguards. His brother, John, remained in Wicklow aiding Lord Baltinglass in his revolt. Towards the end of August, Lord Grew took over the position from Pelham as military commander of the Crown forces, while Bourchier was entrusted with the affairs of Munster.

Once again, the army under Grey headed into Kerry and laid waste to the territory from Castleisland to Dingle, killing everyone. During this time, Admiral Winter was still patrolling the Kerry coast waiting for a supposed Spanish invasion. He seemed to have been a civilised man and did not allow any barbarities from his men ashore. When anchored at Tralee, he negotiated with the people of Tralee to garrison and hold the town for the Queen to avoid any further slaughter.

On the 13 September 1580, a fleet of ships arrived at Smerwick harbour. They had been sent by the Pope and consisted mostly of Italians, but also some Spaniards and Irish. They brought with them a proclamation nominating the Earl of Desmond as papal lieutenant-general of Ireland and Sir John Desmond as commander of the army. For some unknown reason, neither the Earl nor his brother joined up with the landing force, but the English, recognising the danger, moved quickly. Winter, with his ships, arrived early in November and began to bombard the small fort from the sea. Colonel Grey had already surrounded the fortification and was laying siege. After a short period, the besieged force surrendered under certain conditions. After everyone was disarmed, Grey ordered that everyone that was in the fort be killed.

When word filtered through of what had happened at Dún an Óir Fort, the Earl of Desmond raised a considerable force and managed to carry on a type of guerrilla warfare, harassing the English forces wherever they marched. During the following months, the losses on the English side, due to sickness and combat, were substantial. In 1583, the Duke of Ormond changed sides and took charge of the English forces in Munster, and by the end of that summer the revolt was over. Continuously on the run, the Earl of Desmond's camp was finally located and he was beheaded. His head was taken to Cork while his body was interred but moved from place to place, in a bid to avoid it being found by the English.

The adventurers and the newly arrived English moved in fast when the Desmond lands were confiscated in 1584 by an Act of Parliament in Dublin. Most of the lands were held by landlords who could prove that they had no involvement in the rebellion, so only about two hundred thousand acres were confiscated. Sir Walter Raleigh and Herbert received about forty thousand acres and tried their utmost to gain further territory. O'Connor Kerry lost most of his land, including his castle at Tarbert.

Meanwhile, while the intrigue and lust for land continued, Desmond's wife, Elinor, and her daughters were living in abject poverty, until Queen Elizabeth granted her a pension of £200 per annum while two of her daughters received approximately £50 per annum.

*

We now enter the era of the 'undertakers'—those English Protestant families and farmers with money—who were eager to come to Ireland with their tenants, labourers and servants and settle. In addition to these were those who wanted to amass lands. One of these was the Brown family. Sir Valentine had profited greatly already in Kerry and now the two sons of the second Sir Valentine were as avaricious as their forefathers. Thomas Brown gained all the family lands in County Limerick, while his brother Nicholas gained the lands of the MacCarthys and the O'Donoghues, which included the castles at Molahiffe, Castlemaine and

Ross. By inter-marriage, the Brown family kept a hold on the lands that they had acquired, despite some unscrupulous officials who were intent on defrauding every landowner, regardless of whether they were Anglo-Norman, English or Irish. Amongst these were the Herberts, who settled in Castleisland, the Dennys who gained Tralee, the Conways of Killorglin and the Blennerhassetts at Ballyseedy. Other minor families were the Chutes of Tralee and the Crosbies of Ardfert. But the most noted of all was Richard Boyle, who acquired land by questionable means. He eventually became Earl of Cork and an extremely wealthy man and was almost matched by Patrick Crosbie and his brother, who gained possession of great tracts of land in Kerry.

Following the death of the Earl of Desmond, the territory of north Kerry and the county of Desmond were entrusted to the Earl of Clancarre, MacCarthy Mór, who had not taken part in the rebellion and had stayed loyal to the Queen.

Anxious to acquire the lands of O'Donoghue, which were confiscated in 1586, he made representation to the Crown and was successful. He then pledged them to Browne, together with the castle and lands of Molahiffe, Ballycarbery and Glanerought. When Clancarre died in 1596, he left four illegitimate sons and a young daughter called Ellen. Clancarre wanted his favourite son, Donnell, to succeed him. Browne signed a contract to marry Ellen and inherit the title and lands. But Ellen had other ideas and married her distant cousin Florence MacCarthy Reagh in Muckross Abbey in the dead of night. Much argument and animosity followed. Ellen's mother was blamed for the intrigue, as well as Ellen's foster father Donal O'Mahony, who ended up in prison in Castlemaine. Florence was captured and sent to the Tower of London where he remained for about five years, until the summer of 1593. The dispute continued, with both Donnell and Florence claiming the title and an inquisition was requested, just like the inquisition into the claims of Donal Cam O'Sullivan and Sir Owen O'Sullivan as to the title of O'Sullivan Bere which was taking place at roughly the same time.

A few years earlier in 1588, rumours were rife of a great invasion being prepared in Spain for either Ireland or England and both countries were in a state of suspense. Daily life was interrupted by further rumours of imminent invasion, with every official watching the sea for the sign of ships. But when news arrived in Ireland that the Spanish Armada had been defeated off the south coast of England, there was a sigh of relief on the part of English officialdom.

The Geraldines did take part in the Armada in the person of James Fitzmaurice Fitzgerald, who was aboard the *Duquesa Santa Maria,* as well as many other Irish. Unfortunately, he died of fever some time after the ship left Spain.

Having made their way around the north of Scotland, a number of ships found themselves in severe, storm-force gales from the south-west, which drove them towards the west coast of Ireland. A group of about six ships sheltered in the Shannon, not far from Carrigafoyle Castle, before resuming their long journey back to Spain. Three ships were seen in distress in Tralee Bay on 17 September. One of them hit a rock and the crew managed to swim ashore, where they surrendered to Lady Denny, but her husband Sir Edward Denny ordered that they all be killed.

On 10 September, a number of Armada ships came into the Blasket Sound. Juan Martinez de Recalde had been shepherding a small fleet of thirteen or fourteen ships since the third week of August in very bad weather, while maintaining contact with the larger fleet to the west. Losing contact with the main flagship, he broke off and, with some twenty-seven sails, tried to make his way southwards off the coast. In the severe storm during the second week of September, the little fleet was broken up. Recalde in the *Galleon San Juan*, headed for the shelter of the Blasket Islands. He had been there previously when he landed the Italian and Spanish force at Dún an Óir in 1580. Before he reached his destination, he was joined by another galleon called the *San Juan Bautista*, the vice-flagship of the squadron of Castile, which had lost her foremast and was been blown towards the coast.

Having no pilot aboard with knowledge of the Blaskets, the captain followed in Recalde's wake. The two ships anchored off the beach of the Great Blasket in a heavy swell with makeshift anchors. They were so close together that they continuously clashed against each other. They had been anchored for a week, awaiting a lull in the weather and taking on drinking water from the island's wells, when the *Santa Maria de la Rosa* approached through the northern channel. She was firing signal guns to indicate that she was in trouble. Dropping her only anchor she took up a position near the other two ships, but some hours later, with the strong ebb current, she began to drag her anchor and, before her foresail could be hoisted, she rapidly sank with all hands, except an Italian cabin boy. No doubt the captain had intended to manoeuvre the ship away from the nearby Stromboli reef. The cabin boy was washed ashore clinging to a piece of flotsam where he was captured by the English troops, who were keeping watch on the mainland. He was interrogated and then put to death.

At about four in the afternoon, one of the galleons of the Castilian squadron entering the sound was identified as the *San Juan of Fernando de Hora*. She was in a bad state and sinking but somehow managed to slip her anchor, which fortunately held. The weather was so bad with heavy rain that signals could not be passed. Early the following morning, with a relative lull in the weather, the other two *Juans* took off everybody aboard before she went to the bottom and then they commenced their long journey back to Spain accompanied by another pinnace.

According to existing Spanish records, no other person managed to get ashore save the Italian boy. We can only surmise what would have happened if there were other survivors or what were the conditions aboard the great ships, with the remaining food putrefied and only fresh water from the Blasket Mór to survive on. It is reputed that the Irish of the locality collected a fair amount of flotsam in their curraghs when the weather improved. Pieces of this wood can probably still be seen in the houses of the locality.

In 1598, O'Neill rose in rebellion and within a month Kerry fell into rebel hands as the English planters and adventurers fled to Cork. Molahiffe Castle, which was in the hands of the Brownes, withstood an attack for some time while the great castle at Castlemaine withstood a siege for almost a year. Most of the displaced Irish regained their confiscated lands and castles. Sir Thomas Roe Fitzgerald's son claimed the title of Earl of Desmond, which was confirmed by O'Neill as he himself was by now the king of almost all of Ireland.

In February, Lord Mountjoy arrived in Ireland and became Lord Deputy while Carew was given the title of Lord President of Munster. Mountjoy immediately set about the task in quelling the rebellion in Munster. Within a few months, Waterford, Tipperary and Limerick were regained and he then moved into Kerry.

Carrigafoyle was surrendered after a short siege by O'Connor Kerry. He continued through north Kerry, burning crops and driving off the cattle. Florence MacCarthy was captured and dispatched to the Tower of London. He was soon followed by the 'Sugán Earl', who was betrayed by the White Knight in May of the following year. He was to languish in the Tower until his death seven years later.

Without sufficient artillery, the Irish were at a complete disadvantage and, instead of handing over their castles, they undermined and destroyed them before the English artillery arrived. Seeking refuge in the woods, bogs and mountainous regions, they carried on fighting by making sudden attacks on the English forces before retreating to their hideaways. By this time the rebellion was well and truly over.

The arrival of Spanish ships, first at Castlehaven and then a fleet at Kinsale in September 1601, gave an impetus to the struggle. O'Neill and O'Donnell gathered their armies and marched south. The clans in West Cork and Kerry assembled their fighting men and headed for Kinsale, where they were joined by O'Neill and O'Donnell. The English force that was besieging the Spaniards in Kinsale was immediately surrounded and supplies were cut off. A rash decision was made by the leaders to attack the English instead of starving them out.

Advancing on the enemy at night in rain, sleet, snow and gale force winds, the Irish forces lost their way and, when the English counter-attacked, the Irish forces broke up in disarray suffering great losses. The encounter was a complete disaster.

The Irish army broke up and the clans moved back to Kerry and West Cork to protect their own territories. Donal Cam O'Sullivan Bere was made commander-in-chief of the Irish forces as O'Neill decided to return north and O'Donnell decided to travel to Spain to seek more help. While Carew pursued O'Sullivan into West Cork, Wilmot swept into Kerry and defeated Lord Kerry, taking Lixnaw Castle. Next to fall were the castles of Rahinnane and Castlegregory after the defeat of the Knight of Kerry. After a short siege, Dunboy Castle was taken as well as Carriganass, Oilean Beg and Castledermot.

After some three months of fighting superior forces,

O'Sullivan decided to march to Leitrim with ⟨ Kerry and about a thousand people, including men, and children. Only thirty-three survived the jo⟨ ⟨y. O'Neill, knowing that the struggle was over, submitted to the Crown in March 1603.

In 1604, Brouncker succeeded Carew as President of Munster and the English undertakers were told to return to the lands that they had abandoned during the rebellion. Three of the main undertakers, Boyle, Crosbie and Blennerhassett, continued to amass more land. Crosbie was granted lands confiscated after the Desmond rebellion from Fitzmaurice, Stack and MacElligott in Clanmaurice and Iraghticonnor. Richard Boyle, Earl of Cork, also established himself in Kerry, where he acquired vast tracks of land, which were in the hands of Sir Walter Raleigh, for a mere £1,000. When Wentworth came to Ireland in July 1633, he began to question all those lands that had been acquired by the above as well as those in the possession of the Dennys.

During 1641, another rebellion, partly religious, broke out all over Ireland. Kerry joined in and was soon in the control of the rebels. Some of the old Anglo-Norman families also joined the rebellion. Captain Sugán (Florence MacCarthy) of Ardtully was in command of the forces in Kerry, which was made up of the MacCarthys, Owen O'Sullivan Mór, the O'Sullivans and other minor clans.

Lord Kerry, the Knight of Kerry, at this time was in charge of the county for the English government but departed to England when the fighting broke out.

Castlemaine fell after a short siege, while Pierce Ferriter and O'Donoghue of the Glens laid siege to Denny's castle and Rice's Short Castle in Tralee. After a period of about six months, both castles surrendered on good terms and without bloodshed, which was quite the opposite to what happened when the English took an Irish castle.

Another of the main surviving castles was Ballingarry, which was defended by Colonel David Crosbie. This was under siege in 1645 but was taken with the assistance of three of its defenders. Crosbie was lucky to escape with the help of his nephews, the MacElligotts and the MacGillacuddys. Some three years later, he was made governor of Kerry by Cromwell.

On 23 October 1645, the papal delegate, Rinuccini, landed at Kilmacomogue near Ardea Castle with money and a substantial amount of arms for the Catholic cause. His first night was spent in a bothán near the ruined castle but then he moved to Ardtully Castle before journeying up the country.

He happened to be a relation of the O'Connells, who were the guardians of Ballycarbery Castle. As always, the English forces gained the upper hand and the rebellion was slowly and painfully coming to an end. English fortifications went up in Kenmare and on Valentia Island.

In 1652, the siege of the last outpost of Irish resistance commenced; namely Ross Castle on Loch Lein. Knowing that it was almost impregnable from land, Ludlow, who was in charge of the English forces, brought boats by sea from Kinsale and, with the help of bullocks and his own soldiers, pulled them up the river Laune to the lake, like Moriarty had done some four centuries earlier. Even though there were two thousand men behind the walls, it was decided to surrender, seeing that the fortress was about to be attacked from the lake. The terms agreed were that all the defenders would leave the country and a Captain James Nelson was placed in command of the castle. Some local resistance continued but all knew that the cause was lost. Nobody knew what horrors would befall them when Cromwell commenced his strategy of eliminating 'the Irish problem'.

Introduction

The years of the castles and the castle builders were now drawing to an end.

Most of those bastions of power were falling into ruin regardless of who occupied them. The old Irish clans had almost disappeared, as well as the once powerful Anglo-Normans, who had become more Irish than the Irish themselves.

Cromwell's ultimate solution for Kerry was to banish all the Irish from the county and settle them in Clare. He also introduced transportation to the West Indies, especially Barbados. Sources state that over six thousand children were sent to the sugar plantations of that island.

Cromwell's campaign in Ireland was mostly financed by merchants, adventurers and bankers. With the coffers empty on his return to England, he devised a method of repayment by allotting tracts of land to his financiers and those in his army. This was to become known in history as the Cromwellian settlement, where the Irish, the Anglo-Normans, the Royalists and some of the early pre-Reformation English settlers lost everything.

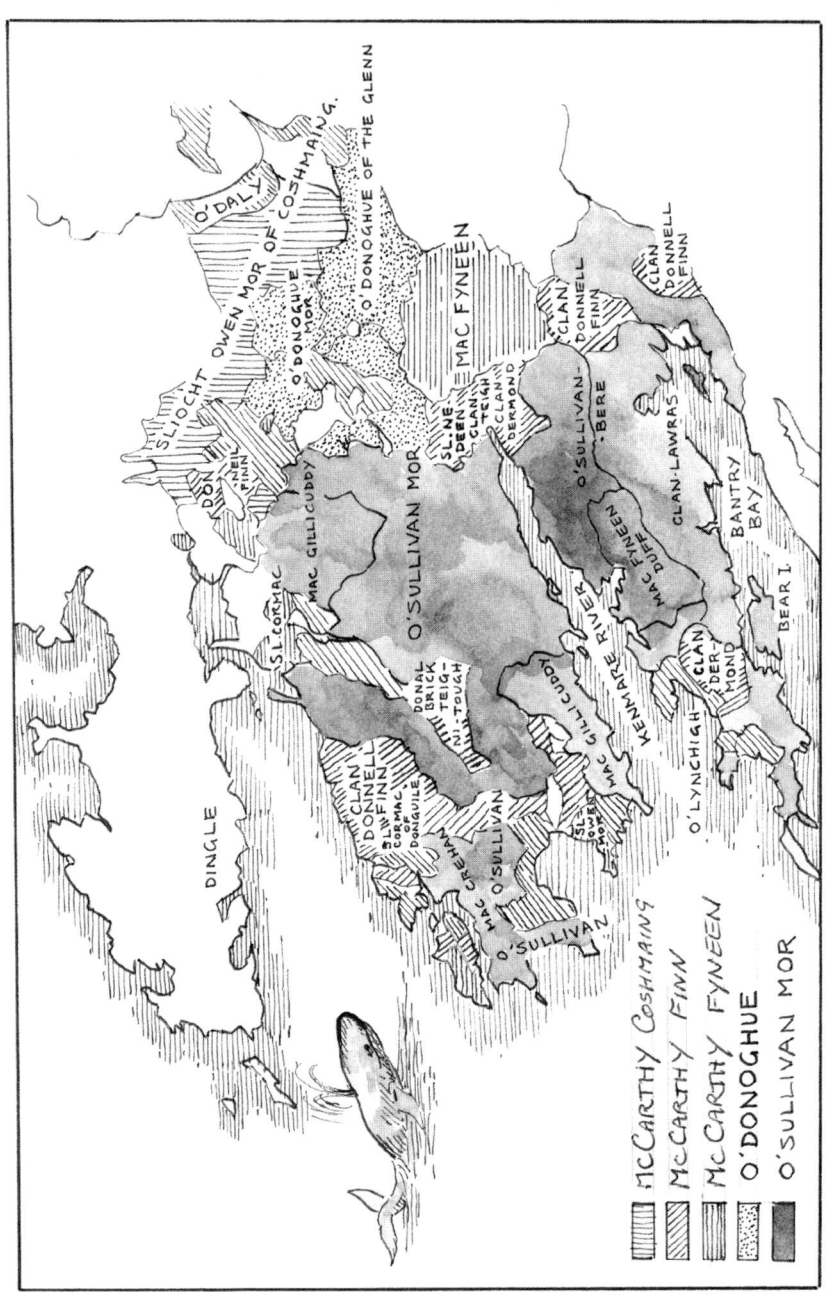

Aghadoe Castle

Parish: Aghadoe: Achadh-Dá Eó—field of the two yews
Townland: Parkavoneen
3 kilometres west of Killarney
O.S. map 78 ref 934 926

This location has also been called Parkavonear by Leask. *Agh* and *dogh* both signify fire. A*chadh-doe* is the field of fire and the *Annals of Innisfallen* mention *Acadh-deogh na greine,* meaning 'fire-field of the sun'.

The Castles of the Kingdom

AGHADOE.

This would indicate the probable usurping of a previous religious site (used for sun worship) by Christian religious buildings (i.e., a round tower and cathedral) at this site.

O'Riordan says it means the place of two yews: *Acadh-da-ca*, 'the field of the two yew trees'. Windele says the round tower is called 'The Pulpit' or 'The Bishop's Chair' (1849). It is possibly thirteenth century and one of the small number of circular keeps in Ireland. Barrow Castle (q.v.) was another.

Sited within an almost square earthenwork, which is defined by an earth bank and fosse, Aghadoe Castle is situated on high ground near Lough Leane, beside an early medieval monastic site and a ruined round tower. Nearby are two embankments. With walls over two metres thick, the building originally had three storeys. The keep encloses an area 6.4 metres in diameter. The ground floor entrance is similar to some castles in south Tipperary, which indicates an early Anglo-Norman castle. An intra-mural staircase connected the ground floor with those above. Evidence indicates there were wooden floors and mural chambers. The fireplace on the first floor indicates where the hall was situated. Windows are oblong on the outside, splayed and arched on the inside.

Quoting the *Annals of Innisfallen*—'In the year 1010 Mael-suthain O'Carroll, King of the Eoganacht of Loca Lein, and chief sage of Ireland, died at Aghadoe.' Also, the church at Aghadoe is reported to have been finished in 1158, so there was probably already a fortification as well, later replaced by the circular stone keep.

Ahalana Castle
Na hAtha Leathana
Parish: Murhur, Tarbert
Townland: Moyvane

The exact location of this castle is unknown. No ruins remain but it was reputed to have been situated on the banks of the Leitrim river beside the bridge on the Tarbert/Listowel road (i.e., Leitrim Bridge).

The castle was built by the O'Connor Kerry clan, probably to defend the boundaries of their terrritory. The district of Moyvane-Knockanure was part of the family heritage of the O'Connors of Carrigafoyle Castle. They built at least two castles in the area, including Glenalappa, some 6 kilometres north-east of the present village and Ahalana.

Nothing else has been passed down in history.

Arabella Castle
MacElligott's Castle
Parish: Ballymacelligott: Town of the MacElligotts
Townland: Arabella

The MacElligotts were Scottish knights descended from the MacClouds of the Isle of Skirth, who came over to Ireland. It is reputed that they came to Ireland with Geoffrey de Marisco, an early Chief Justice of Ireland.

They built three castles within a circle of a mile or so in this parish, which is about 5 kilometres from Tralee: Carrignafeela to the north, Arabella to the south and Bernagrillagh on the west. In the centre of the townland of Arabella are the bare ruins of a castle, with little remaining except indications of the foundations and a section of a wall some 30 feet in length and about 12 feet in height (O'Donovan).

Arabella Castle was almost totally demolished in the eighteenth century. No further facts are known as to its demise.

There are some later references to a manor house built by the Blennerhassetts in 1740–50.

Ardea Castle
See cover illustration
Ardea, Hugh's Height, Baile an Tuosist
Parish: Tuosist: Tuath O'Siosta—territory of the O'Siosta (ancient tribe)
Townland: Ardea
O.S. map 84 ref 774 627

The castle stands on a cliff face overlooking Kenmare Bay at the mouth of the Clonee river. All indications are that it was a substantial building, built from large blocks of green stone and well grouted. Due to its ruinous state it is impossible to make out its size. Some parts of the walls still remain but they are about to fall into the sea due to erosion. From personal examination over twenty years ago, I found that the walls were over 2 metres thick and it seemed that the lower floor was divided into three apartments and there was access to the dungeons, which I was fearful of entering. Some ancient sources say it was a castle of twin towers, plus a banqueting hall, and on a par with Dunboy Castle, but this cannot be verified.

Tradition gives the name Ardea as meaning the 'height of Aodh or Hugh'. This name derives from Aodh Beannan, an ancestor of the Moriartys who had his ancient residence and fortifications here. He was once King of West Munster before the family were vanquished and subdued by the O'Sullivans. Ardea Castle was often referred to as the mansion house of the Moriartys, the original owners, who gave up this castle, and Castle Drummond in the parish of Kilgarrylander, to the O'Sullivans and became their tenants.

The first O'Sullivan who occupied the castle was Philip, brother to O'Sullivan Bere (Cnocanti or Diarmuid of the Powder). He was brother to Owen O'Sullivan of Carriganass, near Bantry. The O'Sullivans were tenants under MacCarthy Mór. This Philip did not join his relatives at the battle of Kinsale, with its disastrous aftermath, and so was able to hang on to his lands when other O'Sullivan properties were forfeited.

Major Philip O'Sullivan of Ardea Castle followed James II to France. His eldest son emigrated to America in 1723, probably to escape implication in the Jacobite plot. One of this man's sons, James Sullivan, became Attorney-General for the state of Massachusetts, an office subsequently achieved by both his son and grandson in turn.

Part of the castle was still habitable when it was occupied by the Coote family from *c.* 1738 to 1756. It was later occupied for a time by a Gill family.

Ardfert Castle

Short Castle (Caislean Gear), Arda Castle
Árd Fhearta—the height of the grave—Cluainfeart Caislean Gearr Arda Ferta
Parish: Ardfert: Árd Fhearta—height of the grave
Townland: Ardfert

In 1253, Thomas, Lord of Kerry, founded a Franciscan monastery on a previous religious site. He was buried there with the previous lords of Kerry and their families. The original castle of Ardfert was situated east of Ardfert Cathedral. In 1312, Nicholas Fitzmaurice is said to have built this castle, though others say it was built by the O'Connor Kerrys.

This original castle was either replaced or improved in about 1570 by the then Lord Kerry. The castle was besieged in 1580 and in 1582 it was attacked twice more by Thomas Fitzmaurice, while the English were in occupation. The English were forced to abandon the castle after the second siege. The town of Ardfert was destroyed by the forces of Maurice Stack in 1599. Now in the hands of the Fitzmaurices once again, it was besieged by Sir Charles Wilmot in 1600 and was captured when Wilmot borrowed a saker (a small cannon) from an English ship. After the garrison surrendered, some men were hanged but the women and children were spared.

Patrick Fitzmaurice, Lord Kerry, rebuilt the castle in 1637. During the Cromwellian wars he was forced to abandon the castle in 1642. The castle was burnt to the ground a year later by a Captain Patrick Lawlor.

No ruins remain.

Note: Barrington: Ardfert Monastery was burned in 1152 by O'Cuilein, burned again in 1179 and plundered by the

MacCarthys in 1180. Innisfallen was raided in 1158, 1160 and 1180 by the O'Donoghues. There was no excuse for the Irish chieftains of the area to sack and plunder the monastery except for their own gains.

Ardnagragh Castle

Parish: Ballincushlane/Ballycushlaan: Baile an Chaisleain—town of the castle
Townland: Cordel
Location: east of Castleisland
O.S. map 72 ref 06 07

This castle was built by the Geraldines (Fitzgeralds) as a fortalice to defend the pass into O'Keeffe territory in County Cork. This was the major route into County Cork up until the nineteenth century. There is no record as to its size or construction, but it must have been a formidable castle as it was always garrisoned and defended by the Fitzgeralds.

Close by is the traditional burial place of the Fitzgeralds, which is called 'Kil-na-nAinm' or church of the name, because only people who bore the name of Fitzgerald were buried there.

The decapitated body of the last Earl of Desmond was brought to the family graveyard some eight weeks after his death. The body was hidden in a small recess at Glaunageentha wood until it was safe to remove it.

It is said that, in the nineteenth century, a stone coffin thought to contain the remains of the Earl was dug up in the graveyard. It was later broken up and used in a lime kiln.

Ardtully Castle

Parish: Kilgarvan: Cill Garbhain—church of St Garvan
Townland: Ardtully: Árd Tulac—high knoll
Location: 3 kilometres west of Kilgarvan

This castle is located about 3 kilometres west of Kilgarvan, close to the confluence of the Roughty and Owenbeg rivers. The castle was built by Carew *c.* 1215, not far from where the decisive battle of Callan was later to take place. It was taken by MacFyneen MacCarthy in 1261 after that engagement but was reoccupied by English forces a year later. Partly destroyed in 1653 it was known as Finin MacCarthy's mansion and the MacCarthys occupied it for almost four hundred years. In 1641, the whole parish belonged to Colonel Donough MacFyneen and to Dermod MacFyneen MacCarthy, except about 900 acres belonging to an Edmund MacMole Murray, who does not belong to any of the major clans. Later, the Cromwellian forces attacked the castle and the MacCarthys forfeited the castle and lands. At this time, the property also included two houses, a corn mill, tuck mill, malt house, barns, a silver mine and an iron mine. These were granted to a Captain Dillon but they were later passed on to the Hollow Blade Company of London to pay off debts incurred by Cromwell. A Mr Conway became occupant of the castle and lands *c.* 1702, then, some fifty years later, a Mr Orphen was in possession.

    A descendant, a Mr William Orphen, built a new house on the old castle site. It was a Victorian house with two wings and a large turret with battlements in the centre.

    In 1641–2, Donagh MacFeinnine Cartie of Ardtully was one of the besiegers of Tralee Castle. In 1645, the Nuncio, Archbishop Rinuccini, landed at Kenmare Bay and stayed at Ardtully Castle before commencing his journey to Kilkenny. Donagh MacFeinnine entertained the Papal Nuncio,

Rinuccini, Prince of Fermo, with twenty-two Italians after they had landed near the castle of Philip O'Sullivan at Ardea. Donagh was married to Catherine, the daughter of Lord Muskerry. It is not known why the Papal Nuncio and his party were moved up to Ardtully from the relative luxury of Ardea Castle, with its great hall and well-appointed accommodation.

Note: Carew, or De Carraun, was one of the early Anglo-Norman invaders from Wales. He was originally from France but married into a Welsh family and was related to the Fitzgeralds and other early Anglo-Norman invaders.

He is reputed to have built a number of stone castles, including Ardtully, Dunamark near Bantry, Dunkerron on the Kenmare river, Cappanacushy, Callownafersy, Castle Cois Mainge, Molahiffe, Clonmellane and Fieries.

Donal MacFinnan fell at the Battle of Aughrim and over three hundred Kilgarvan men died at Slane Ford at the Battle of the Boyne.

Astee Castle
Asdee Castle—Caislean Easa Dubh
Townland: Astee
Location: Aghavallen, Ballylongford

The castle was built outside the village of Astee, which is about halfway between Ballylongford and Ballybunion.

In ancient sources it was described as a minor castle of the O'Connors of Carrigafoyle Castle. According to the *Annals of Innisfallen* it was built by Diarmuid Sugach O'Connor c. 1150. According to the unpublished notes of one Ned Moriarty, it is stated that two walls existed at right angles to each other and were 20 feet high and over 6 feet thick. He also mentioned that there was the possible remains of an arch but this was covered in ivy. Stones from the castle were used to build nearby houses.

In the seventeenth century, the castle was the home of Sir Anthony Edmunds, whose wife was a daughter of the O'Connor Kerry. This saved the Astee lands from confiscation and the estate remained in the Edmunds family until 1812.

Ballinanig Castle
Ballyneanig Castle
Parish: Marhin: Marthan: Paraiste Mharthann
Townland: Ballinanig/Castlequarter

Caislean Bhaile an Aonaigh or Neanaig was named after Neno O'Connor, who lived in the castle. It was situated about 5.5 miles north-north-west of Dingle. This tower house was located on the south side of Smerwick harbour, somewhere just east of Ballyferriter village. It may have been built in the mid-seventeenth century and was occupied until 1810.

What remained in 1841 measured 9.14 by 7.62 metres internally and the wall thickness was 2 metres. The stairway was situated in the south-west corner. The ruins were about 6.1 metres high. Twenty years later, the stones were removed to build houses and now nothing remains.

The castle is reputed to have been built by the O'Connors and later occupied by the Ferriters but, according to Lewis, it was built by one of the Desmonds and later occupied by Moriartys.

Ballinskellig Castle
Skellig Castle
Parish: Prior: Paraiste an Phriora—parish of the prior
Townland: Ballinskellig
O.S. map 83 ref 435 655

The castle is situated on the west shore of a bay, a short distance from the priory.

This was a small castle built on an isthmus to defend the harbour against pirates, according to Smith in his *History of Kerry*. It is situated about a quarter of a mile from the famous Abbey. The ruins measure about 33 feet by 25 feet and the walls are about 6.5 feet thick.

The doorway is on the south wall and inside to the left is the spiral stairway inside a sort of round tower. Reaching the first floor, there is a passage running through the south wall. The inside of the tower is completely destroyed. To the right, on entering the doorway, is a small room referred to as the Chamber of the Rustic (Seomra an Bhoduig). It seems that the castle had only two floors. Nothing but the bare lower walls remain and it now suffers from sea erosion.

As far as is known, this was supposed to be a MacCarthy Mór castle. The date of building is not known but it must have been an early watchtower to protect the harbour from the many pirates ships off the coast during the fifteenth and sixteenth centuries.

Ballinskelligs Church was used by the monks that survived the Danish raids on Skellig Michael. After the confiscations under Elizabeth I, it passed with the adjoining land to a Roderick Harding of Bristol and later passed to Sigerson and Mahony of Dromore. The monastery was founded in 950. It is interesting to note that King Olaf of Norway, while in exile, was reputed to have been baptised a Christian in 995 on the Skellig or in Ballinskellig Abbey.

Ballingarry Castle
Leap Castle

Ballingarry: Baile an Gharraí—townland of the garden
Parish: Ballyheigue: Baile Uí Thaidhg—town of O'Taidgh
Townland: Cloughaneleesh—the stone of Ellish
Location: 2 miles north of Ballyheigue
O.S. map 63 ref 759 332

Ballingarry Castle was also known as Queen Elizabeth's Fort.

The castle was said to have been built *c.* 1585 by Thomas D'Cantillon. The site had been associated with the name of D'Cantillon since the thirteenth century.

It was granted to George Isham and was refortified by Gerrot Roe Stack, who was the brother-in-law of Lord Kerry.

The site was fortified by Colonel D Crosbie in the war of 1641, for the defence of the narrow isthmus leading to a small peninsula where his English tenants could shelter from Irish attacks and be supplied across the Shannon by friends of Lord Inchiquin. The garrison of Tralee retreated here after the fall of the Great Castle in 1641. It was taken through the treachery of a servant in 1642, when one called Kelly let the drawbridge down to allow the Irish to enter. Crosbie was in bed with an attack of gout and did not realise what was happening until alerted by a lady of the household.

He defended his chamber until he was allowed to surrender, after which he was taken to Ballybeggan. There was a plot to murder him there but he was rescued by two nephews, who were both colonels in the Irish army. This illustrates the closeness of relationships on both sides of these wars.

The chasm between the mainland and the isthmus later

became know as 'the tailor's leap', from a story about a tailor who anxiously waited for news of a newborn child and, when he heard that his wife had given birth to a boy, jumped across the open chasm in a fit of joy.

There are some ruins remaining, including the base of a turret, earthworks, souterrains and the castle itself. The outline of the ruins of some houses can be seen.

Ballinruddery Castle
Trant Castle
Parish: Finnogue: Fionnuig—crow
Townland: Ballinruddery or Baile Trant
Location: 2 miles east of Listowel
O.S. map 64 ref 017 335

The tower castle stands in ruins on a cliff face. Situated on the south side of the river Feale. It was probably built late in the fifteenth or early in the sixteenth century.

All that remained in 1841 were almost all of the east wall, the south wall and most of the north wall. The west wall has been completely destroyed and not even the base remains. It is not possible to give the dimensions of the castle. The original walls were over 50 feet in height and 7 feet thick, with some ten square windows. No floors or stairway survive and it is impossible to say whether it had four or five storeys. There are a number of fireplaces on what was possibly the second floor, plus indications of others.

A corner bartizan on the north-west corner is found over halfway up the wall. It is a small roofed machicolation with slots for muskets and openings in the floor to throw down missiles on any attackers who might try to dislodge the bottom cornerstones of the castle. There is no evidence of a bawn wall. However, there is possible evidence of earthen ramparts west of the castle.

It is reputed to have been built by the Fitzgeralds, the Knights of Kerry, early in the fifteenth century, who were connected by family ties to the Earls of Desmond. About 1579, one of the Fitzgeralds, John, was declared an outlaw and rebel, but he was later pardoned. The castle was granted to Sir William Herbert by Elizabeth in 1588.

After 1601, the lands were forfeited and then, after the Cromwellian wars, they fell into the hands of Eaton and Power, who were paid in land for services rendered. The Fitzgeralds finally repossessed the castle and lands in 1742.

The castle is now within the demesne of Ballinruddery House.

Ballybeggan Castle

Parish: Ratass: Ráth Teas—southern fort
Townland: Ballybeggan
Location: close to the racecourse, about 3 kilometres north-east of Tralee
O.S. map 71 ref 863 155

This was formerly a strong military fortress and before 1639 it belonged to Walter Hussey. It may have been built by the Husseys or given to them by the Earls of Desmond.

During the rebellion, from 1641, it was held for the English by Richard Exham. He had gained possession when the castle and lands were mortgaged to him by Hussey only a few years earlier. In or maybe before 1649, it passed to a Colonel Crosbie. The castle endured a long siege in 1641 when attacked by an Irish force under Florence MacCarthy, Maurice MacElligott and the Walter Hussey who had been in possession a few years before (see old Kerry records, p. 283).

The castle was defended by Exham, who made many attempts to try and lift the siege on Tralee Castle. In 1643, the castle was relieved by Lord Inchiquin's forces.

During the war of the revolution, it was burned by the Irish. By the end of the seventeenth century, the castle had been sold or leased to the Morris family and, by 1756, it was in ruins and the owners occupied a new mansion nearby.

It is recorded by Smith that close by this castle were some orchards and that, beneath, there was a system of interconnecting caves that had a stream flowing through them in which trout and salmon could be caught.

Ballybunion Castle
Bunion, Bunyan and Buinnean Castle
Parish: Killahinny: Cill Eithne—church of St Eithne
Townland: Ballybunion: Baile an Bhuinneanaigh—town of the family Bunion
O.S. map 63 ref 864 413

Situated near a cliff face overlooking the white strand of Ballybunion, it seems that this castle was built within an enclosure—probably an old promontory fort. Nothing now remains, only the east side wall, which was over 60 feet high and 7 feet thick. It is possible that the entrance was in the east wall, as well as some five windows. In the south-east angle of the tower there was a spiral stairway, which, unusually, turned from right to left, but no steps exist today. There are indications of a pointed arch on the top floor, and according to Westropp (1909) there were vaults over the lower and middle

floors. In the 1980s, a man-made escape tunnel built of stone was discovered running from the cliff face to the castle. This souterrain may be associated with the earlier promontory fort and would have been incorporated by the castle builders at the planning stage. It seems that the original building measured 26 feet from north to south and 13 feet from east to west on the inside. The doorway is placed on the east side. Ballybunion was called after a man named Bunnion.

The castle was built by the Fitzmaurices in the fourteenth century and served as the abode of the heir apparent of that family until the middle of the sixteenth century. The castle was destroyed by Lord Kerry in 1582. It was taken over by the Bunnion family, who were retainers of the Geraldines in west Limerick. They were at first custodions and eventually came into possession, but they got involved in the Desmond wars and the castle and adjoining lands were confiscated. The castle and lands were handed back to Thomas Fitzmaurice by King James in 1612.

The Fitzmaurices held on to their possession at least until 1690. However, the castle and lands came into the possession of Richard Hare *c.* 1783 and the Hare family held on to the castle and adjoining lands until *c.* 1923.

Not far north are Pookeeneen and Doon castles.

Ballycarbery Castle

Parish: Caher: Chathair—stone fort
Townland: Ballycarbery
Location: near Doulus Bay, Cahergeal—Chathair Gheal—the white stone fort
O.S. map 83 ref 447 798

This castle was built on a slight eminence on the tidal estuary of the river Ferta, just east of Valencia harbour. It is said that it was built by Carbery O'Shea using the blood of bullocks to cement the stones.

Originally, the very sizeable fifteenth-century castle consisted of a main hall house with a projecting tower at a north-east angle surrounded by a bawn. The main castle itself measures about 62 feet by 43 feet. The other tower measures about 12 feet by almost 7 feet. A stairway extending to the top of this 60-foot main tower gives access to the rooms of the other part of the building. The ground floor of the main castle was divided into three parts under arches. Over the two eastern arches was the main hall and at the western side was another room. The walls were over 9 feet thick.

It is not a typical hall house and has some aspects of a tower house. It was taken over by the O'Sheas *c.* 1400, who gained possession of the territory from the O'Falveys. MacCarthy Mór brought the O'Sheas to task and installed a family of the Clan O'Connell under Morgan Dubh as constables. These O'Connells were ancestors of Daniel O'Connell.

There is a legend that indicates how independent these constables could be. MacCarthy Mór is supposed to have sent a cradle to O'Connell as an indication that he would send a child for fostering. O'Connell cut off the messenger's head and sent it back in the cradle. MacCarthy had the bearer of this message hanged. Filled with anger, MacCarthy Mór came with a large army, took the castle and hanged

The Castles of the Kingdom

BALLYCARBERY CASTLE

Morgan Dubh from the highest window. It is reputed that on a certain night of the year, Morgan's screams can be heard echoing around the castle walls.

The castle is said to have been destroyed by Ireton, Cromwell's son-in-law, during the Cromwellian invasion.

Ballycarnaghan Castle
Ballycarna Castle
Parish: Kilcrohane: Cill Crócháin—church of St Crohan
Townland: Ballycarnaghan
Location: about 1.5 miles east of Derrynane and south of Caherdaniel
O.S. map 83 ref 549 589

This was a small tower house built on a rock and reputed to have been constructed early in the seventeenth century.

It measures about 38 by 26 feet and the walls are over 6 feet thick. The doorway was on the east side and the spiral stairway was located in the north-east corner. Its height cannot be judged as the remains are now only about 15 feet high. It was built by the Formoyle family, who were relations of the O'Sullivan Mórs.

Ballycarty Castle
Parish: Ballyseedy: Baile Ó Sioda—town of the Sheedys
Townland: Ballycarty: Beal atha Caerdcha—forge ford

This tower house was a Geraldine fortress in 1580. It was used by the Irish forces in 1641 during the siege of Tralee. It is situated about 4 miles east of Tralee. Ballyseedy Castle, located nearby, is a much later structure.

Ballycushlane Castle
Kilmurray Castle, Ballycushlaan Castle
Parish: Ballycushlane: Baile an Chaisleain—town of the castle
Townland: Kilquane
O.S. map 72 ref 057 097

The ruins of this old tower house, which gave its name to the parish/townland, are extensive. It consisted of a court and two towers, with one attached to the east end and the other attached to the south-side wall.

The length of the ruin, including court and tower, is 48 feet. The height is about 45 feet and the walls are over 8 feet thick. There is a chimney on the west wall and two fireplaces remaining. On the east wall there are two or three

Kilmurray Castle

fireplaces. On the south-side wall of the court there are two rows of windows and three opposite on the second floor.

There were three floors in the court and the tower, which measured about 16 by 12 feet, at the east end of the castle, while on the north side there are four windows.

Kilmurray Castle was reputed to have been built by Meiler Fitzhenry *c.* 1200, after he was granted the northern part of the county by King John.

The castle and lands were later reputed to belong to a Fitzgerald—one of three brothers who were always fighting amongst themselves. The other two brothers lived in Ballyplimmoth Castle and in Ballymacadam, which were situated within a half mile of each other. They hated each other and would not let one another pass unmolested through their lands. There is some confusion over the number of Fitzgerald castles in this area. Some sources also mention Kilcushnan Castle and, if Ardnagragh is taken into account, the total comes to five castles within 6 kilometres east of Castleisland, all very close to each other.

The castle was taken over by a Colonel Thaire in 1650.

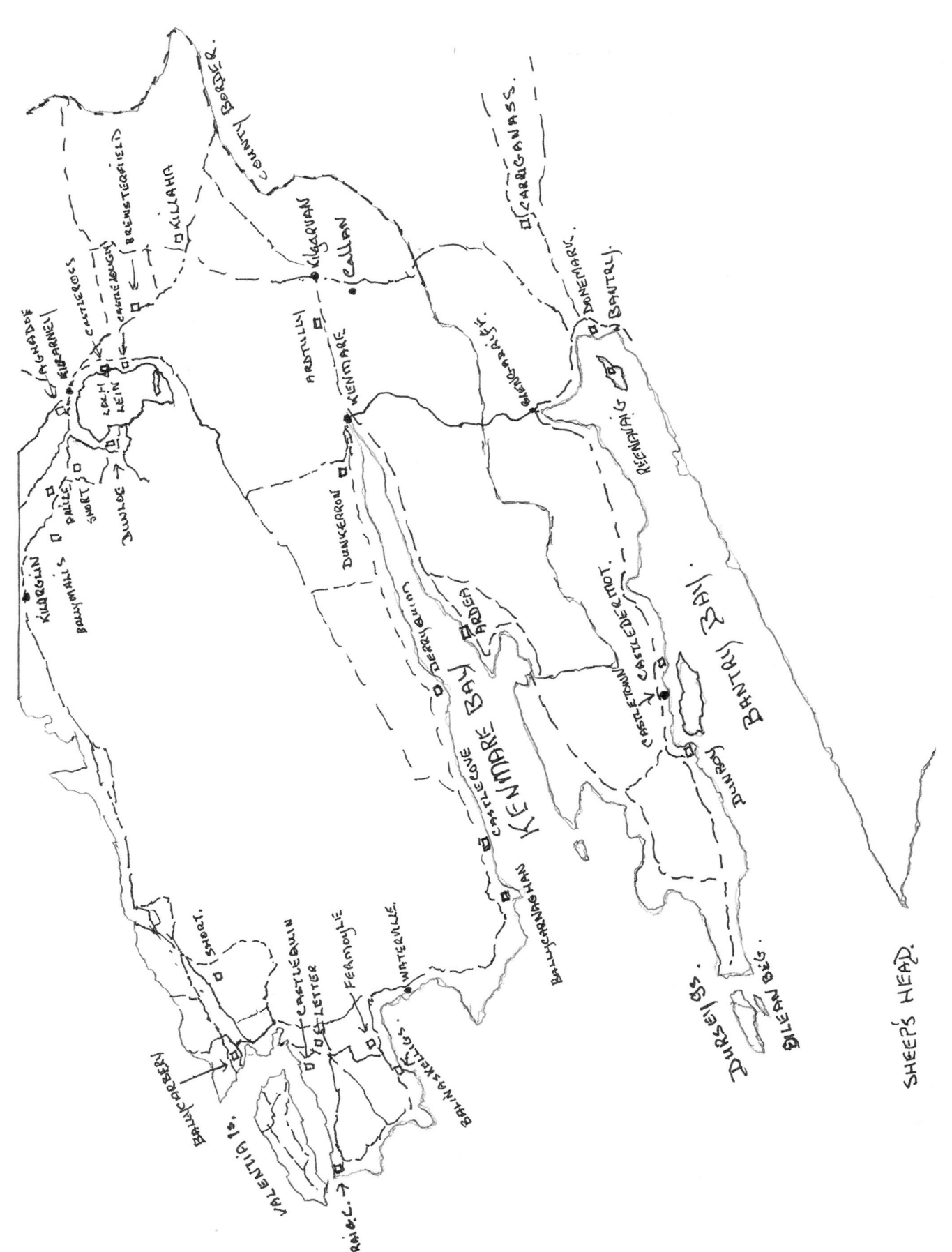

Ballygrellagh Castle
MacElligott's Castle of Bernagrillagh (Ballygrillaghe Castle)—Ballingrillach/Ballingrilough

Parish: Ballymacelligot: Baile MacElligott—town of the MacElligotts
Townland: Ballygrellagh: Beal Atha Greallach—mouth of the Miry Ford
Location: 8 or 9 kilometres south-east of Tralee on the Killarney road
O.S. map 71 ref 898 112

The ruins of this tower house stand on the south-eastern corner of the townland, 5 miles from Tralee. On the inside, the castle measures at its base 20 feet by about 14 feet and the walls were about 7 feet thick.

It seems to have had narrow windows. The third floor was built over a stone arch and the doorway was on the west side, which was larger than normal, measuring 7 feet in height and 4 feet in width.

The MacElligotts were strong landlords in these parts and were descendants of the famous MacCloud Clan from the Isle of Skye in Scotland. They were probably Scottish mercenaries or adventurers who came over with the Anglo-Normans.

The ancient lands of the MacElligotts were between Tralee, Listowel and Castleisland. Mary MacElligott was the wife of Maurice Fitzmaurice in 1297 and brought three townlands as a dowry.

In 1584, Ulick MacThomas Elligot of Carrignafeela held Baile MacElligott and Tullygarron. These were granted to Sir Thomas Roper in 1613. In 1588, Morris MacElligott held Ballygrellagh Castle.

Three castles are within a circle of 3 miles in this parish: Carrignafeela to the north, Arabella to the south and

Bernagrillagh to the west. All originally belonged to the MacElligotts.

Ballyheigue Castle
Parish: Ballyheigue: Baile Uí Thaidhg—town of O'Taidhg
Townland: Ballyheigue

Tadgh D'Cantillon built the first castle some distance away from the present site of the third castle. A remnant of this structure survived as a strong tower during the time when the second castle was occupied. This was a long, low stone building of considerable size and with a thatched roof of the 'old type'—something like Dunkerron Castle on the Kenmare Estuary. The third house, founded in 1758, was mentioned by Lewis in 1837 as 'the seat of Colonel J Crosbie. It was a superb structure in the later English style of architecture, erected after a design of Mr Robert Morrison and situated in an extensive demesne'.

In October 1729, the Danish ship, *Golden Lion*, was driven ashore on Ballyheigue Strand. She had on board about £20,000-worth of silver bullion. This together with the other salvage was removed to Ballyheigue Castle for safe keeping or as bounty. The silver was removed in an armed raid in 1731 by the Irish. In 1441, Edmund, son of Maurice D'Cantillon, Lord of Ballyheigue, was named in a charter. All the D'Cantillon lands and castle were forfeited in 1651. Chevalier Antoine D'Cantillon was created Baron of Ballyheigue by Louis Philippe in France.

From earliest times, the D'Cantillons buried their dead on a small island out in the bay, where there was an ancient burial ground and a ruined church. The island disappeared under the sea in a great storm. Fishermen related how, on a calm day, they could see the walls of the old church and the tombs and always blessed themselves and said a few prayers for the dead, to avoid a watery grave. The old legend of the D'Cantillons related that, if any of the D'Cantillon family died, their coffin would be left on the seashore and, by the following morning, it would have been taken by the tide to find its own place in the burial ground beneath the sea, or else carried by the sea people (sea fairies) chanting an eerie funeral song.

The castle and lands were given to the Crosbies during the confiscations under Queen Elizabeth. Soon after their occupation of the castle, they became known as shipwreckers and smugglers. They used to leave their horses to graze near the shore at night with lanterns tied to their necks and, when the horses' heads bobbed up and down, anyone at sea would think that the lights were of another ship and come closer to the shoreline. Many ships were wrecked and stripped of their cargoes and their crews put to death.

Ballykealy Castle
Baile Uí Chaolla
Parish: Kilmoyly: Cill Nhaoile—church of St Maoile
Townland: Ballykeighly: Baile Uí Chaolaighe
Location: about 6 kilometres north of Ardfert
O.S. map 71 ref 792 278

There is no evidence of this castle visible today, but there are signs of the moated site on which it was built.

According to O'Donovan in 1841, what remained of the castle measured about 20 feet on the east-west wall, and what remained of the north wall was about 16 feet high with a thickness of over 7 feet.

The castle belonged to a minor branch of the Fitzmaurice family. According to the *Annals of the Four Masters* (1577), this castle was taken with a number of other castles, including Ballykealy, by MacMaurice, who was marching south to Kinsale with O'Donnell in 1601. No definite date is given. The castle is also mentioned in the *Four Masters* in 1582 and in 1601.

It should be noted that O'Donnell was far west plundering, instead of hurrying to Kinsale to assist the Spaniards who were besieged. The castle, amongst others nearby, belonged to the Fitzmaurices. According to Smith, the castle was one of the main residences of the Fitzmaurices. Later it became the seat of Maurice Crosbie, but it changed hands again in 1736 when Sir Robert Fitzmaurice took possession.

Ballymacadam Castle
Bally Mac Adam
Parish: Ballycushlane: Baile an Chaislean—town of the castle
Townland: Ballymacadam
O.S. map 72 ref 039 096
See also Kilmurray and Ballyplimmoth castles in this context

Kilmurray, Ballyplimmoth and Ballymacadam castles were all situated within half a mile of each other and were inhabited by three Fitzgerald brothers of the Desmond family. They hated each other and would not let each other pass unmolested through their lands. Kilmurray Castle was the major building of the three.

There is some confusion over the number of Fitzgerald castles in this area. Some sources also give Kilcushnan and, if Ardnagragh is taken into account, that comes to five castles within 6 kilometres east of Castleisland, all very close to each other.

What little remains is in the grounds of the eighteenth-century Ballymacadam House.

Ballymacaquim Castle
Baile Mic an Cahaim—Pierce Castle
Parish: Killahan: Cill Laiathain—church of St Liathin
Townland: Ballymacaquim: Baile Mic an Chaim—town of the son of a stooped man
Location: about 4 kilometres north-north-west of Abbeydorney in the townland of Ballymacaquim East
O.S. map 71 ref 829 264
This was a tower house

Built on high ground, this castle had a commanding view of the surrounding area. The remaining part at the south-east angle is about 55 feet high, but the stairway at this corner has fallen apart. The ground measurements are about 34 feet by 25 feet. The remains of a vault can be seen over the second floor. The doorway was on the north wall and the remains of a fireplace can be seen on the west wall. Mounds of earth can be seen nearby, which may have been for defensive purposes.

The castle was probably built by the Fitzmaurice family but no date can be given. In 1303, Pierse Fitzmaurice was in possession of the castle and it became the main seat of that family, who became known afterwards as the Pierses. This branch ceased to exist in the mid-1700s but a number of families still bear the name. The castle is mentioned in the *Annals of the Four Masters*. It seems that the Pierses built a new castle on the site of an older castle. Later, some of the descendants fell into dispute about the ownership of the castle and the Earl of Desmond was drawn into the conflict. The Earl took over the castle and, soon after, the young Abbot O'Torna was shot at Lixnaw Castle. During the ensuing conflict, many of the Fitzmaurice family were killed or drowned when they tried to escape the carnage.

Earlier, during the absence of the one of the Fitzmaurices and his men, a woman who was staying at the castle allowed a number of men to enter. They got inebriated and pursued her around the interior looking for her favours. Reaching the top chamber and realising that she had no escape, she went to the window on the west wall and jumped to her death to avoid being raped. It is said that her terrible screams as she fell to her death could be heard on each anniversary of that night while the castle stood. Maybe her ghost still inhabits the ruins.

Some years later, Reginald Acham, who was in charge of the castle, promised to give his daughter to one of the Browns in marriage. However, she had already pledged her love to a dashing young local chieftain called MacSheehy. It came to pass that both Brown and MacSheehy were invited to a feast in the castle. When Sir Reginald and his family had retired, MacSheehy was drugged and removed to one of the chambers. Brown and his men came into the chamber later in darkness and one of them slashed down with his sword on where he thought MacSheehy's head rested. But Mac-Sheehy had been lying the wrong way around, with his legs on the pillow. With the victim screaming in agony, he was immediately smothered and stabbed and his body removed from the castle.

When Brown returned to the chamber later to remove the bloody bed covers, he found that the legs had not been taken and they were immediately thrown out of the window into the moat below. The daughter, thinking that she had been abandoned by her lover, waited for months for his return. With her father pressing, she finally agreed to marry Brown.

Some time later, the wedding between the daughter and Brown took place and a large wedding feast was held in the castle. During the course of the celebrations, silence descended as a horse was heard coming across the drawbridge. Everyone began to wonder who the late guest might be. A few minutes later, the door to the large hall suddenly flew open and everyone screamed in fright and bewilderment as two severed legs in boots plodded across the floor and came to rest in front of a vacant chair opposite the bride and groom. Everyone scattered and tried to get out of the hall. Then there was utter consternation when out of the boots grew a body, shrouded in a kind of mist, and everyone remaining immediately recognised the young MacSheehy. The bride let out a piercing scream upon seeing her lover. Brown tried to stand up, clutching at his throat and gasping for breath, and eventually he fell down dead on the floor. After surveying the gathering, the apparition stared longingly at the bride and then vanished as the two legs began to walk back to the door. A few minutes later, the sound of horses' hooves could be heard crossing the timber drawbridge and fading into the night.

After this event, the young bride never left her chamber and spent her time weeping and screaming until, one day, she threw herself out of the window to her death, knowing that the father of her new husband was the cause of her lover's death.

Ballymalis Castle

Parish: Kilbinaun: Cill Beanain—church of St Benignus
Townland: Ballymalis: Béal Átha Málais: Baile átha magh lis
Location: about 7 kilometres east-south-east of Killorglin
O.S. map 78 ref 840 938

This ruined castle stands over the river Leamhain (Luane) and measures about 50 feet by 30 feet. Its walls are over 8 feet thick and about 55 feet in height. Towards the east there is a cross wall, which divides the building into two very unequal parts, making the eastern part look like a tower and the other part like a dwelling house. There are three arches in the eastern part on which the three lower floors would have rested, and a spiral stairway in the south-east corner, which is in good condition. The doorway was in the east wall. This section of the castle has sixteen windows. The castle had four storeys and many apartments. It is supposed to have been built by the O'Moriartys but it is also known as Ferris Castle. There were many interesting features about this castle, including a good

Michael J Carroll

BALLYMALIS

example of machicolation, which is dated to the sixteenth century—a small roofed machicolation with slots between the corbels and some musket loops in the walls. Inside there is a small L-shaped room which is approached by a passage in the corner of one of the upper rooms of the castle. In addition, there were two bartizans at second-floor level to prevent an enemy from undermining the corners.

At approximately the end of the sixteenth century, the castle was completely changed and rebuilt. It was then in the possession of the Ferris family, who were responsible for the defence of the territory. Before that it was in the possession of a minor sept of the MacCarthys.

The castle experienced many sieges and attacks and was confiscated in 1677. Murrough MacOwen Ferris of the castle was subject to confiscation and transplantation to Connaught *c.* 1653. In 1656, the castle and lands were in the possession of Sir Francis Brewster. They were later forfeited, in 1677, and the Eager family took possession.

Ballymullen Castle
Castle Morris
Parish: Ratass: Ráth Teas—southern fort
Townland: Ballymullen: Baile an Mhuilinn—townland of the mill

This castle was also referred to as Castle Morris and was situated on the southern outskirts of Tralee, near the river and the railway. This was another Desmond castle and belonged to a branch of the Geraldines known as the MacRoberts of Trughenackmy, who were descended from Nicholas, youngest son of the first Earl of Desmond by his third wife Elinor Fitzmaurice. In the Inquisition of 1622, the castle and lands are mentioned as the former lands of Thomas Fitzgerald's MacRobert's castle.

Very little of the castle remains except for parts of the north and south walls, about 12 to 15 feet high. The spiral stairway ran through the south wall and the third floor was built on a stone arch. Nothing is visible today, except a corner and a mound of rubble.

Ballynoe Castle

Parish: Killury: Cill Luraigh—church of St Lurach
Townland: Ballynoe
Location: very close to Rathmorrel, about 3.2 kilometres from Causeway
O.S. map 63 ref 797 302

No trace whatsoever remains now of this castle, which was once held by the Brown family, then later by a branch of the Stoughton family, who arrived as planters in the late sixteenth century. An eighteenth-century house, built on the approximate site, later passed into the hands of the Pierce family.

Ballyplimmoth Castle

Parish: Ballycushlane: Baile an Chaisleain—town of the castle
Townland: Ballyplimmoth
Location: about 4 kilometres south-east of Castleisland
O.S. map 72 ref 045 090
This castle was a tower house

The castle, once four storeys high, is now in complete ruin. It was built on limestone rock beside a river, constructed using lime and sand mortar, and square blocks of limestone laid in regular courses, which were grouted. It is said to have had caverns and caves beneath. The north wall is at the water's edge. The castle seems to have been about 17 by almost 14 feet at the base and had a stone arch inside. The doorway was on the south-east corner wall.

There were two other small castles of the Fitzgeralds in this area, occupied by three brothers who were always in dispute with one another.

There is some confusion over the number of Fitzgerald castles in this area. Some sources also give Kilcushnan and, if Ardnagragh is taken into account, that comes to five castles within 6 kilometres east of Castleisland, all very close to each other.

No further details are available at this time except that the castle was always caught up in the various Desmond rebellions.

See Ballycushlane (Kilmurray) and Ballymacadam.

Barrow Castle

Parish: Ardfert: Árd Fhearta—height of the grave
Townland: Barrow
Location: the northern side of Barrow harbour 4.5 kilometres south-west of Ardfert
O.S. map 71 ref 725 184

There was a round castle here commanding one side of the harbour entrance, with Fenit Castle on the other side. The castle had a diameter of 30 feet and was at least two storeys high with a spiral staircase. The seventeenth-century Barrow House stands on, or near, the original site, as its back walls are about 7.5 feet thick.

Barrow harbour, which was navigable in ancient times, was guarded by three castles—Tawlought, which has disappeared, the tower house at Fenit and the round tower of Barrow.

One of the old legends of the area states that gold from a Spanish Armada ship, wrecked along the nearby coast, is said to have been buried at Barrow Castle and guarded by a mysterious black watchdog, which was frequently seen at night. This story was told to Tourist Authority researchers by some of the local people in the 1940s.

Beal Castle
Bialle Castle—Viale Castle—Beaulieu Castle
Parish: Kilconly: Cill Chonnla—church of St Connla
Townland: Beal or Castlequarter: Ceathru an Caislean—castlequarter
O.S. map 63 ref 909 484

This castle was built near the back of sand dunes on the shore, where the tides once came within 20 feet of the walls. It has an excellent view domineering the Shannon river and has also been referred to as Beaulieu Castle in the *Pacata Hibernia* (1633). Only the south-west corner wall of the castle remains now. This is about 50 feet in height and some 6 feet thick. From Westropp (1909) we learn that the tower had two floors under a vault and another storey was vaulted, with an additional room overhead which was roofed. Little remains today but indications of the foundations. From the ground works, it appears that a rectangular enclosure, measuring approximately 210 feet north to south and 218 feet east to west and about 20 feet thick, was an additional fortification as a fosse.

This was one of the Fitzmaurice castles. It is reputed to have been built some time during the thirteenth century. On or about 1307, Gerald Fitzmaurice received the castle from his father. However, he was dispossessed by his half-brother, Pierce. Gerald never regained the castle. In 1581, the fortifications were destroyed by Patrick, Lord Kerry himself, to prevent the castle being used as a fortification for the English.

Facing defeat at the hand of the English forces under Carew, Thomas Fitzmaurice, eighteenth Lord of Kerry, sued for peace but his plea was rejected by Carew. Following the death of Maurice Stack, a lifelong friend of Carew, Fitzmaurice was declared an enemy of the Crown. There are various versions of how Maurice Stack was lured to his death by Honora O'Brien in the castle; whether he was stabbed to death by her in her quarters or someone else did the dirty work, nobody will ever know.

Morris Stack—brother of John Rice was murdered in Beale Castle in 1600, reputedly on the orders of Lady Kerry. His brother Thomas was hanged the following day by order of her husband, Lord Kerry and Knight of the Glen (i.e., Thomas Fitzmaurice, also called the Sugán Earl).

One of the tales related to the castle is that the ghost of a vicious black dog guarded the castle. Nobody in later years ventured near the castle at night. Edmund, Lord Kerry, died at Beale Castle in 1549 after the battle of Knockanure.

It is said that the famous pirate queen, Grace O'Malley, on her return journey to Ireland—after meeting Queen Elizabeth at Hampton Court on the Thames—anchored her vessels offshore to take on supplies of food and water. Recognised as the 'pirate queen' who had previously attacked and removed the cargoes of wine, brandy, etc., which were destined for the castle, she was apprehended and placed in the dungeons with a number of the landing party. When notice of her situation was passed to her ships, the crews immediately came ashore and, after a short encounter, released her, as well as all the other prisoners that were being held. She then continued her journey home to her base at Clare Island, off the coast of Mayo, after giving a full broadside to the castle, warning that she might return.

Another tale is that, when the castle was besieged by English forces, the lady of the castle went out to take a walk in the castle grounds for fresh air. By chance, she encountered the commander of the besieging army and, after a long conversation, she invited him to a meal in the castle, where he would be in no danger and nobody else would appear except her servants. He accepted her word for his personal safety and entered the castle the following night on his own. During the meal he noticed that one of the servants had a knife hidden in the folds of her dress. Realising that there was something amiss he rose from the table and drew his sword. Immediately all the servants threw off their garments revealing that each and every one of them were armed young men. With all the doors locked he retreated up the spiral stairways knowing that he was completely outnumbered. Arriving at the top parapets he was overcome and thrown over the wall to his death. It is said that the lady of the castle regretted her deceitful action and that she went mad. When she eventually died, her ghost, dressed in a white dress, was reputed to have been seen walking the parapets of the castle on many occasion in expiation of her hideous crime.

Bebhion Castle
Leck Castle—also called Lick or Lickbebune Castle
Parish: Kilconly: Cill Chonnla—church of St Connla
Townland: Faha-an Fhaighe
O.S. map 63 ref 862 450
Also, in olden times the castle had other various names, i.e., Fhehanaleca, Faitce na Lice (graze of the flagstone), Lic Bebhfionn, Bevan's Castle, and Bebhionn's Castle (we understand that Bebhionn was a woman's name)

This castle is located on the extreme south-western part of the parish, on a high cliff called Leck point, otherwise known as Lackfevun, over the mouth of the Shannon river. It stands on a point of rock or a headland, which was about 350 feet long. It was cut off from the mainland by a gap cut into the rock. Access was originally over a natural arch, but when this collapsed, access was then over a timber drawbridge. Access now is by a narrow path over the fallen rock into the chasm. The south wall of the castle still remains and is over 30 feet high and about 7 feet thick. The wall was part of the tower which contained three storeys. Other sections of walls, which existed a few centuries ago, indicated that this was once a fine castle of considerable size. The impression given was that of a substantial tower house with additions. It was built by one of the Clan Richard of Leac Beibhionn c. 1380.

John, son of Garret Fitzgerald and heir to Leck Castle, was killed during the siege of Lord Kerry's castle at Lixnaw in 1568. The castle was demolished prior to 1641. It is mentioned in the *Annals of the Four Masters* in 1582 as one of the castles of Lord Lixnaw.

James Fitzjohn Fitzgerald forfeited the castle and lands c. 1608. The castle was in ruins by this time. Near the ruins is a columnar cliff known as the Devil's Gate—see Devil's Castle (Doon Castle).

Note: Blasket Mór watchtower

Various references were made as to an early castle on the Blasket Mór by some earlier writers. After research, it was ascertained that a stone-built watchtower, with two storeys, was built in either the fifteenth of sixteenth century to alert the authorities of a possible French invasion. The watchtower was located above the old village on the slope, with a view of the south and north channels and the Sound.

It was probably similar to the two watchtowers that were built on Valentia Island, one guarding Ballinskelligs harbour, and others built along the West Cork and Kerry coastline. They were probably abandoned and in ruins by the time people first began to live on the island.

Brewsterfield Castle

Parish: Killaha: Cill Átha—church at the ford
Townland: Brewsterfield
Location: about 10 kilometres south-east of Killarney in the valley of the Flesk river
O.S. map 79 ref 045 875

No details or history can be located on this castle, except that it was probably an outpost of the O'Donoghues.

The castle was dismantled in 1652. About a hundred years afterwards, a house was built probably on, or near, the ruins of the castle. Nothing exists today.

Brown's Castle

Parish: Killoory: Cill Luraigh—church of St Lurach
Townland: Clashmeelcon: Clais Mhaolchion
Location: 6 kilometres due north of Causeway village
O.S. map 63 ref 815 366

The ruins of this castle stand on the edge of a cliff. It is located in an old promontory fort. Parts of the east wall only remain. It seems that it was built of slate taken from the cliff face. Built over 60 feet high, it measured 33 by 20 feet at its base. The doorway was on the east end, some height above ground level. A spiral staircase existed in the south-east corner and a stone arch stood over the second floor. The castle was separated from the mainland by a narrow trench, and for additional defensive strength, two walls ran back at angles from the trench to the stronghold.

The castle was more than likely built by the Brown family in the middle of the fifteenth century. These Browns, or

Brouns, were an Anglo-Norman family who were engaged in piracy and smuggling from the many caves situated beneath the castle. They were in occupation of the castle from c. 1220 to 1584.

Sir Reginald was sheriff and Sir Gilbert was guardian of Tralee in the thirteenth century.

Westropp stated that the castle had three floors with a vault over the second floor. Colman refers to the existence of the entire upper floor in 1871, and the lower was used as a shelter for cows.

One legend associated with Brown's Castle is that of a black devil dog who protected the access to the door.

Also, mentioned in relation to the castle was the tale of a king named Lynch, who was known as Cluas Capaill. He was possessed of the ears of a horse but protected his secret by the expediency of having each barber who cut his hair executed.

Burnham Castle
Ballingoleen Castle
Parish: Dingle: Daingean Uí Chuis—fort of O'Cuis
Townland: Burnham
O.S. map 70 ref 422 998

The castle was situated on the Burnham peninsula, south-west side of Dingle harbour, not far from Ventry harbour where Colaiste Ide now stands.

It was once a seat of the Rice family, before the wars of 1641 and later belonged to the Mullens family.

Near here, a very large old brass spur was found deep in a bog. Smith, in his *History of Kerry*, says that it had probably belonged to a Knight Templar, and was at the time he wrote, in the possession of Mr Mullens.

The Templars had possessed land in this area until it was forfeited by the Fitzgeralds (see Foley p. 178).

The name Burnham was given to the land by Colonel Frederick Mullens. He named it after his birth place in England.

Little remains now except for a few stones. We have no idea of the structure of the castle but more than likely it was a square tower house like the other castles located in that part of Kerry. It is reputed to have been built by the Rice family who were an early Norman family; however, there is no date of construction.

It is recorded that one of the Rices, called Piers Rice, built a castle at Smerwick on an outcrop of rock. James Desmond later cut a piece out of the rock measuring about 40 feet in length and about 20 feet broad and 20 feet deep to make its position stronger. It was later referred to as the 'Island of Ardcanny'.

There is a mention of Peter Rice of Smerwick and Dingle *c.* 1579 and it is related that a Captain John Rice, who was acting as pilot, died of fever aboard one of the Armada ships after leaving Spain in 1588.

The Rice family seem to have been in possession of their castles and lands up to 1641 and carried on until at least 1656 when a Dominic Rice is mentioned. The lands and castle were confiscated in Cromwellian times and were handed over to the Countess of Mountrath *c.* 1666. The lands were resold a few months later to a Mr Mullins. This family eventually acquired the title Lord Ventry.

Caher Castle
Shangarry Castle
Parish: Kenmare: Ceann Mara—head of the sea
Townland: Caher: Caislean—castle

Lewis (1837) says that the foundations of a castle were visible at Caher parish in Kenmare and, in 1841, O'Donovan found only a fragment of wall.

Callownafersy Castle
Callan na Feirse—Cala na Feirse
Modern spelling: Callinafercy
Parish: Kilcolman: Cill Colman—church of St Colman
Townland: Callinafercy: Caladh na Feirse
Location: was between the outflows of the rivers Maine and Laune, west of Miltown
O.S. map 71 ref 780 003

A castle was built here in AD 1215 by Maurice Fitzgerald. It was a fully fortified Norman castle. Nothing remains today and no further details survive.

Camp Castle

Parish: Killgoban: Cill Goban—church of St Goban
Townland: Camp
Location: 16 kilometres south-west of Tralee
Sometimes referred to as Cahirmoreaun or Bongoinder. Later changed to Camp

This castle was supposed to have been located north of Curraduff bridge, about 16 kilometres south-west of Tralee. It was probably built by a branch of the Fitzgeralds. Further up the valley is Glandine Castle.

In 1871, Cusack describes scattered remains, to the left of the road from Tralee to Dingle, on an elevated site.

There is also a question about the existence of a second Camp castle. This was supposed to have been located about a mile further west on the right-hand side of the road, near an ancient graveyard. No local folklore exists today referring to its existence.

Cappanacushy Castle
Cappa na Couse

Also called Coss Castle or Cappanacosse
Parish: Templenoe: Teampall Nuadh—new temple or church
Townland: Dromore
Location: between Kenmare and the Blackwater, 6 kilometres west of Kenmare
O.S. map 84 ref 835 692

This castle belonged to a minor branch of the O'Sullivan Mór family, who were known as 'An Sliocht Macrah'. They had the right of chieftaincy if the main branch of O'Sullivan Mór should have no male heirs.

The location of the castle is now in forestry plantation. The ruins stand about 2 miles from Dunkerron Castle. It was built of green stone and limestone. Only the east wall and a small portion of the south wall existed in 1841. There are indications of stone arches inside the east wall—one over the ground floor and the other over the third floor. The castle had four storeys. Measurement of the south wall indicates that it was over 35 feet. There is no indication as to the other dimensions. The walls varied between 5 and 6 feet in thickness.

The castle was reputed to have been built by Carew and then belonged to a younger branch of the O'Sullivan Mórs, MacGrath MacRait, brother to O'Sullivan Mór. The castle was supposed to have been the official residence of the Tánaiste of the O'Sullivan Mórs while Ardea Castle was held by the Tánaiste of the O'Sullivan Bere. With little or no land to survive on, the O'Sullivans of that branch made their way to foreign lands. The castle remained in the hands of the O'Sullivan/MacGraths from 1261 to 1661. Owen O'Sullivan forfeited the castle and lands during Cromwellian times.

A descendant called Daniel O'Sullivan raised a complete regiment of foot and horse soldiers for Bonnie Prince Charles *c.* 1744.

The MacGraths MacRaith are stated to have been the senior branch of the 'Sullivans at Ceapa na Coise Castle'.

Carrigafoyle Castle
Carrig a Foile
Parish: Aghavallen—ford of the little river bed
Townland: Carrickafoyle: Carrig an Phoill—the rock of the hole
O.S. map 63 ref 987 475

This was the chief residence of the O'Connors. The castle is situated near Baile Longford. It was constructed by Connor Liath O'Connor Kerry after his election as clan chief in about 1490. It is situated on the site of an earlier castle. In 1841, it was described as being in good condition except for the west side.

Built on a rock near an island in the Shannon and surrounded by water, the tower was about 70 feet high and measured about 30 feet by 60 feet. The second and fourth storeys were covered by vaults. Small chambers were built in the haunches of the vaults to reduce weight. The door was situated on the east side and above the high water mark. A spiral stairway at the south-east angle gave access to the upper floors. The doors of the upper rooms, giving access to the stairway, were situated in the corners and fitted into recesses in the walls.

There are openings of various designs using lintel stones with relieved arches. Other unusual features were the columbarium at the end of the curtain wall, which completely surrounded the courtyard, and a small boat dock at the foot of the tower.

The castle was defended on the land side by double walls, the outermost having square flankers measuring about 50 feet by 15 feet while the inner had round bastions. The area between the two bawns was used as a dock for boats, while the island at the back defended it from attack by sea. The keep measured 60 by 30 feet in plan and was 95 feet high. It had six storeys, two resting on stone arches, constructed

CARRIGAFOYLE

from chiselled limestone. In 1841, three sides remained with about forty windows and 100 feet in length of outer wall, 12 feet high.

It was the main stronghold of the O'Connors of Kerry until they forfeited their castle and lands in 1666.

The castle was attacked by Queen Elizabeth's forces under Sir William Pelham on Palm Sunday, 1580. Artillery fire-power was brought into use for the first time in Kerry. Pelham set up cannons on the mainland to the south and placed ships on the Shannon and so the bombardment commenced. The castle was stormed after two days. It is said that the defending garrison consisted of fifty Irish, including some women and children, one Englishman, and sixteen Spaniards under the command of an Italian engineer, Captain Julio. Modern cannons were brought in by English ships under Admiral William Winter, but these did not make much of an impression at first. However, the English had aid from within. An English officer had begun an affair with one of O'Connor's maids and arranged for her to place a light in a window at the spot where the walls were weakest. This she duly did and the attackers concentrated their armaments on the west gable, which eventually gave way after a long bombardment. A breach was made in the wall and a Captain Mackworth, with his men, entered and took over the castle. Sixty of the defenders found inside were immediately put to death, including the young woman who had betrayed the defenders.

With the castle taken, Pelham marched some of the forces to Lislachtin Abbey. Most of the monks sought refuge in the woods but those that remained were put to death and the monastery was ransacked.

Later the O'Connors regained possession. John O'Connor married Julia, a daughter of O'Sullivan Mór. He rebuilt part of the damaged castle, but then, in 1600, John O'Connor (known as O'Connor of the Battles) surrendered Carrigafoyle to Sir George Carew.

John O'Connor rose up and regained his castle on hearing the news of the arrival of the Spaniards at Kinsale. He united his forces with those of O'Sullivan Bere at Castlehaven, and then with O'Neill and O'Donnell at the battle of Kinsale. After the defeat, he retreated with what remained of his army. Sending most of them home, he himself was to become one of the heroes of the famous march to Leitrim and happened to be one of the very few survivors. He visited King James in Scotland, and was favourably received. James arranged for John O'Connor to be reinstated at Carrigafoyle. He lived until 1640 and died at Tralee at a very old age. He had no living son, and his daughter Mary married her cousin Conor Cam O'Connor. She died without children and Donagh O'Connor took over the chieftainship.

In 1649, Carrigafoyle Castle was captured by the Cromwellian army and was almost totally destroyed.

In 1666, the Carrigafoyle and O'Connor Kerry estates were forfeited to Trinity College Dublin under the Act of Settlement. This was the end of the O'Connor dynasty.

Further Information
c. 1151—Mahon O'Connor married Johannah, daughter of O'Moriarty of Loch Lein, and Diarmuid O'Connor married Marie, daughter of Roderick O'Donoghue Mór.

In 1169, the O'Connors lost a great part of their territory when the Anglo-Normans took over and became their overlords, later to become the Earls of Desmond.

In 1200, the O'Connors moved to Carrigafoyle and built their chief residence. They moved there from their smaller castles of Astee, Tarbert and Ahalana.

John O'Connor was chieftain in 1451. He married Margaret, daughter of David Nagle of Monahinney. They had the monastery of Lislachtin built for the Franciscan monks and this was completed in 1478. John died in 1485 and was buried within the monastery. He was succeeded by his son Conor who married his cousin Johanna, a daughter of Sir Edmund Fitzthomas Fitzgerald, Knight of Glin.

In 1490, Conor commenced the work of building a new castle on the site of the old family castle. This is the strong castle mentioned after this date. Conor died c. 1523. His son, Conor the Fair, succeeded him. He, like his ancestors, traded in goods and wine from France and Spain and imposed a toll on every ship passing Carrigafoyle on its way up the estuary to Limerick. He married twice—firstly, to Margaret, daughter of Edmund, Earl of Desmond, and then to Slaine, daughter of Torlough O'Brien of Killaloe.

In Desmond West Cork

Carriganass Castle

Parish: Kilmacomogue: Cill MacComoge—church of young Colman
Townland: Carriganass: Carrig an Easa—rock of the waterfall
Location: just east of Kealkil village
O.S. map 85 ref 048 566

Carriganass was probably built by Dermod O'Sullivan c. 1540. It was one of the main strongholds of the O'Sullivan clan: 'Nulla manus, tam liberalis, et geralis, atque universalis, quam Sullivans.'

This was a lofty four-storey square tower house, perched on a rocky base by the Ouvane river. Its square court, which may be more recent than the tower, was flanked by four round towers and a 14-foot wall. It is possible that Carew constructed the square court, due to the large number of musketry loops in the north and west walls, which indicates the prevalence of gunpowder by that time. The heavy gate entrance was on the north wall, while the inner courtyard had stables and outbuildings on the east side and a keep situated in the west corner by the river.

A small section of the south wall remains and the other three seem strong. The four corner turrets are in reasonable condition, and the castle is generally in a better condition than the other O'Sullivan strongholds in the area.

The O'Sullivans were reputed to have been descendants of Aodgh Dubh (Black Hugh), as were the MacCarthys, and so trace their ancestry back to Heber, the eldest son of Milesius. The name itself derives from one of the early chiefs, Echy, son of Maoliura, who had only one eye and so was called Suil-Amhain, or One-Eyed. During the reign of Elizabeth I, the O'Sullivan clan emerged as two distinct branches: O'Sullivan Mór and O'Sullivan Bere, the first being ranked as chieftain. Their combined territory extended from Dunmanus Bay to Castlemaine in Kerry. Both were bound under allegiance to MacCarthy Mór and were obliged to attend him in battle with sixty horsemen and fifteen hundred infantry. O'Sullivan Mór was also expected to lead MacCarthy's army and to entertain him with all his retenue for two nights a year, or whenever he was in the locality.

The O'Sullivan who built Carriganass was called Dermod and he was also known posthumously as An Phdair (The Powder), having blown himself up with gunpowder. The ensuing family rivalry for the chieftainship caused many deaths, including those of his brother and one of his sons.

Another brother, Owen, took over the chieftainship in 1563 and in 1565 he surrendered his lands to the Queen in a regrant agreement. For his fidelity to the Queen he was knighted. During the Desmond rebellion, however, he sat on the fence and failed to assist the English, who removed him to prison in Dublin as a result. In 1557, during Owen's absence, his nephew Donal Cam (The Limp) contested the leadership and reoccupied his father's castle at Carriganass. He was thrown out when Owen was released from prison, and retreated to Beara. It is reported that, upon Owen's arrival with his guards, Donal was surprised in her ladyship's chamber, and escaped by jumping out of the window into the swollen river below. He was lucky to escape with his life.

Donal wanted the chieftainship dispute settled according to the old Irish Brehon Laws, but Sir Owen took recourse to the English Commission in London. Eventually, in late 1593, an agreement was reached. Donal got everything west of the Adrigole river (the inferior portion), and his uncle retained all the lands east towards Bantry. An illegitimate nephew, called Philip, got a portion of Ardnagashel.

Sir Owen died in 1594 and his son, also called Owen, married one of the daughters of the O'Mahonys of Dunmanus Castle and inherited the eastern domain. He became involved in a bitter rivalry with Donal Cam, now styled O'Sullivan Bere, which deepened when it was rumoured that Donal was conducting an affair with Owen's wife during his absences from Carriganass.

In 1601, the call came to assist O'Neill and O'Donnell, who were on their way to Kinsale to join up with the Spaniards. Donal moved quickly and took Carriganass Castle and removed Owen's wife to Dunboy Castle, while he himself marched his army to Castletownshend in thirty-two hours. Owen's force, meanwhile, was also on its way to Kinsale.

Following the Irish defeat, Donal, now commander of the remaining Irish forces, hastily retreated south, left a garrison at Carriganass and headed to Dunboy Castle to strengthen its defences. Carew was marching south with a large army, capturing most of the Irish-held castles en route. Arriving at Bantry, he encamped at Dunamark and took Carriganass Castle. He also captured Reenavanig Castle on Whiddy Island, where he stationed most of his troops.

After the fall of Dunboy Castle, Carew marched back to Bantry and, leaving a strong garrison at Carriganass, his army marched to Cork. Donal recaptured the castle some time later but it was retaken by the English forces under Wilmot. Not to be outdone, Donal recaptured the castle while Wilmot was encamped at Glengarriff. Facing utter defeat, Donal commenced his epic march to Leitrim. Utterly frustrated, Wilmot, having retaken Carriganass, had all the garrison hanged on their surrender. Now on the English side, Owen occupied the castle for a number of years until he built Reendesert Court, which was a fortified house. A family named Barrett inhabited the castle for many years, until it was purchased by an O'Sullivan in the 1930s. Today it is partially restored.

Carrignafeela Castle
Parish: Ballymacelligott: Baile MacElligott—town of the Elligotts
Townland: Carrignafeela—watch rock—view of the surrounding countryside
Alternative townland name is Tooreen
O.S. map 71 in kilometre square 90 15
See also, Arabella Castle and Ballygrellagh (Bernagrillagh) in same parish

There are three castles within a circle of less than 3 miles in this parish. Carrignafeela to the north, Arabella to the south and Bernagrillagh to the west. All originally belonged to the MacElligotts.

Here we have the site of what was called the Earl's Castle. Nothing except a group of stones remains. It is reputed that, when he was on the run, the Earl of Desmond sought refuge here before he was later captured and put to death by the Moriartys in 1583.

This castle was built by Maurice Fitzgerald in 1216 and was demolished in the nineteenth century.

Arriving back in Kerry after the Desmond wars, Sir Edward Denny, finding Tralee Castle in ruins, moved into Carrignafeela Castle.

There was a large prison accessed through the natural limestone caverns beneath the castle and there are also stories of a 'hanging ring' on the west wall. Maybe this is the same as the 'gibbet' mentioned below.

The most infamously tyrannical occupant was Sean a Cuillig, who may be the MacElligott referred to in the Rev. Brosnan's story mentioned below.

Story from Rev. J Brosnan, PP, quoted by Cusack:

The last MacElligott to hold Carrignafeela would seize passers-by and have them hanged for the amusement of his daughters, whom he would invite out to enjoy the spectacle. The gibbet was kept permanently erected in the courtyard.

Castlecore Castle
MacGillycuddy's Castle
Parish: Knockaun: Cnockane—hillock
Townland: Dromaloughane—ridge of the small lake
Caislean Cor Castle by the round hill
Location: about 3 kilometres west of Beaufort Post Office near a mansion called Churchtown which belonged to Arthur Blennerhassett
O.S. map 78 ref 917 850

The ruins of this castle lie about half a mile south-east of the old church on open ground. Only part of the north side stands. It was originally a square tower house with additions on the south side—maybe a second and smaller tower. It is not possible to ascertain the original size but the existing north wall gives a height of about 60 feet. A very large fireplace can be seen with a chimney stack on the north wall, which would indicate that this part was built late in the sixteenth century.

Castle Cor was also called The Castle of the Marsh. It was built *c.* 1480 by the MacGillycuddys, who were a branch of the O'Sullivan Mór. The MacGillycuddys went into rebellion with the Earl of Desmond in 1583.

Donal MacGillycuddy was killed and his lands were confiscated in the reign of Queen Elizabeth. Barrett took over and later the lands passed to Hussey. In 1598, the lands and castle were returned to the MacGillycuddys. Donagh fought against the Cromwellian forces on the side of Charles I, and as a result lost the castle and all his lands. Somehow, the MacGillycuddys regained Castlecore and some of their lands before 1630. Donagh MacGillycuddy raised a small army of foot soldiers for King James and suffered the consequences in 1641. Donagh MacGillycuddy burned down the castle fearing that it would be taken by the English forces.

The Castles of the Kingdom

CASTLE CORE

Before this, with the aid of a male servant, he removed all his treasure of gold and silver, as well as other booty, and buried them somewhere near the castle before chopping off the servant's head and letting his lifeless body fall into the pit with the treasure. Many people have searched the area for the hidden treasure over the centuries without success. In modern days, people with metal detectors have been seen in the general area searching for the treasure of Castle Cor.

After the Restoration of 1660, Donagh again regained possession of his castle and some of his lands. He became high-sheriff of Kerry in 1687. His son Denis abandoned the castle in 1696 when he married into the Blennerhassetts of Killorglin Castle.

In 1688, Cornelius fought on the side of King James and, along with many of his own soldiers recruited from his territory, was killed at the Battle of the Boyne with the large Kerry contingent defending the ford at Slane.

The family tomb of the MacGillycuddys is in the nearby church grounds near the east gable.

Castle Cove Castle

Bunaneer Castle/Bernaneeve Castle
Caislean Bona an Uidhir: Castle at mouth of Eer river/
Bunaneer Castle/Bun Inbhir
Parish: Kilcrohane: Cill Crócháin—church of St Crochan
Townland: Behaghane
Location: about 16 kilometres from Sneem on the road to Caherdaniel near the Kenmare estuary
O.S. map 83 ref 593 602

The ruins of this square castle are situated on a rock at the southern end of the parish. Very little remains. It probably was never completed.

It measured about 38 feet by 21 feet north to south and the walls were about 5 feet thick. A spiral stairway led to the top of the castle at the north-west corner. There were five windows on the north wall, two on the east wall and one on the south wall. The doorway was located on the west wall.

This was a castle of O'Sullivan Mór and was described as a sixteenth-century tower house. One unusual feature is a kind of string course formed of thin flagstones in an upturned V-shape, looking like the weather mould of a gable on each face. Below this, the walls have a batter, but above it they are vertical, with the result that the string course has hardly any projection at the corners but a considerable one at the apex of each V.

No particular history is available from recorded sources.

Castle Craig

Parish: Killemlagh: Cill Imleach—the church on the border
Townland: Reencaheragh: Reen na Caheragh—mound of the fort
O.S. 83 ref 350 722

The remains of this castle are situated on a headland called Doon Point about 2 kilometres west of Portmagee. The site was noted in Smith's map of 1756, where it is called Reencaheragh.

We know very little about this castle, which had a commanding view over the entrance to Portmagee channel and Valencia harbour. It was surveyed for the tourist authority reports in the 1940s, when a wall 40 feet long and 3 feet thick was recorded and there were indications of a door in the north wall and a nearby gatehouse tower. Jeremiah King states that Reencaheragh was owned by a Dunadh O'Sullivan of Doon Point. The current landowner, as of March 2004, is Johnny Pat O'Sullivan, who is probably a descendant of the original O'Sullivans.

In Desmond West Cork

Castledermot

Townland: Knockaneroe: Cnocan Ruadh—little red hill
Parish: Kilanconenagh: Cill Acha n-Aoineach—church of St Acha of the fasting

Castledermot was situated on a high rock overlooking Castletown harbour from the east, not far from where Castle House now stands. An old illustration depicts a moderate tower house, maybe of three storeys.

Nothing survives of the castle now but Lewis in 1835 stated that he observed some remains of the lower walls. Nearby is a small inlet called Brandy Hall, which was noted for smuggling from France and Spain.

The castle is believed to have been built by Dermod O'Sullivan *c.* 1473. However, there is another theory involving a Dermot Donn (Brown Hair) MacCarthy, who was the brother of Finghin MacCarthy of Ringrone, who was victorious at the Battle of Callan. This would imply that the castle was built much earlier, perhaps around 1260, by the MacCarthy overlords.

When Donal Cam returned from Kinsale, he took up occupation of the castle, as Dunboy was in the hands of the Spanish garrison. During the ensuing siege of Dunboy in 1602, an officer of Donal Cam called Tyrell had the castle garrisoned when Carew arrived on Denish Island. In a surprise attack, the garrison were overwhelmed and the castle taken and this became the main base of the English force. After the fall of Dunboy, Carew ordered that Castledermot be razed to the ground, so that it could be no longer be used by the O'Sullivan forces, who were still at large in the rough terrain of the interior.

Castle Gregory
Caislean Griagaire/Castle Connell
Parish: Killiney: Cill Einne—church of St Ende
Townland: Castlegregory
O.S. map 71 ref 620 135

This is a large castle erected *c.* 1288 by Gregory Hoare (Gregory le Hore) and built of limestone slabs. His son also held the castle (see story in Foley, pp. 84–

5). Later, two Walter Husseys owned the castle from about 1585 until 1641 (see Foley, p. 88), when it was besieged by the Cromwellian forces. Making his escape by night, Walter Hussey took up his position at Minard Castle. When this castle (Minard) was taken by the Cromwellian forces under Colonel Lehunt and Sadler, Hussey's men were blown up by powder placed in the vaults killing most of the garrison that remained. The castle was partially demolished in 1650.

Although the remains were standing in Smith's time (1750s), by 1841 very little was left. Only a few stones remain now. Some stones were used for building houses in Castlegregory.

There are some vague references to Aba Castle and Owen Cashla in Killiney, which might mean the same castle or possibly others which have vanished over time.

Castle Gregory was referred to as the castle of misfortune, as if it were cursed. When Barrett's son, Hugh, prepared to entertain some of Lord Grey's forces on their way to Smerwick—including Spenser, Walter Raleigh and Colonel Zuche—his wife, who did not like the idea of entertaining the English officers, removed all the bungs from the barrels of wine, brandy and port in the cellar. In a fit of anger at being so embarrassed, Hugh killed his wife and the following morning he threw himself off the parapet after his guests had departed.

Castleisland Castle

Parish: Castleisland: Oilean Ciarraighe—the island of Kerry
Townland: Ballymacadam
O.S. map 72
Referred to as 'Castle de Insula'

Approximately a mile and half east of Castleisland town are the ruins of a square castle. Inside it measures about 16 feet by 13 feet. Nothing remains of the spiral stairway which led to the top floor at the southeast corner. The second and fourth floors were built over stone arches. The walls, in contrast to other castles, were only 4 feet thick. The east and north walls no longer exist. The south and west walls still have some lower windows. The older castle on Castleisland was much larger in size but no records exist of its original plan. There was one square tower where, today, the foundation barely exists. The ruins of the later castle measured about 15 by 15 feet and was 45 feet high. This section was but a flanking tower. It had two floors over the gateway with several narrow and small windows which were for defensive purposes.

The former castle is reputed to have been built by Geoffrey de Marisco in 1226. This Geoffrey was a nephew of Strongbow and son-in-law to Maurice Fitzgerald. He became Lord Justice of Ireland in the year 1215. Castleisland passed to the Geraldines through the marriage of Elinor de Marisco, who was either a daughter or granddaughter of Geoffrey. In 1345, the castle was besieged by Sir Ralph Ufford, Judiciary of Ireland, because, at the time, it had held out for Maurice Fitzthomas, first Earl of Desmond. The three knights commanding the garrison, Eustace le Poer, William Grant and John Coterel, were all executed.

It was the largest Irish fortress under the earls of Desmond until 1600 and the chief residence of the Fitzgerald family, whose estates totalled over 500,000 acres. The Earl held his court in the castle without interruption until 1576. It was described in 1580 as 'a high, monstrous castle of many rooms, but very filthy and full of cow dung'.

Castleisland Castle was destroyed in 1660 but was later partially restored. The *Kerry Evening Post* of 31 March 1866 reported that the crumbling walls had fallen in a storm a few days previously. The Fitzthomases were known as the lords of 'The Manor of the Island'.

Following the confiscations of Elizabeth, the area fell into the hands of the Herbert family, who remained in control from 1600 to 1900.

Castlelough
Pool Castle
Parish: Killarney: Cill Airne—church of St Airne
Townland: Caislean an Locha
O.S. map 78 ref 972 883

The castle was located on a rocky promontory on the Lower Lake about 3 km south of Killarney town centre. It lies close to the head of the bay of the same name, between Ross and Muckross Abbey.

It was originally a strong fortress connected with Muckross Abbey. The castle was erected by the MacCarthys and was listed in the possessions of MacCarthy Mór in 1588.

It was granted in 1605 by James I to Donnell, the natural son of Donald, Earl of Glencare, who had previously held possession. In 1641–2, Donnell MacCarthy of Castle Lough was one of the besiegers of Tralee.

The castle was destroyed in the Cromwellian wars and almost completely razed by Ludlow's forces under Colonel

Sankey in 1652. The MacCarthys seem to have hung on to it, however, for some further time after this and it was occupied by a younger branch of the family of MacCarthy Mór. In 1849, Windele would write of only a few vestiges remaining.

Addendum

As a result of a decree of the Court of Claims in London on 28 July 1663, the lands of Palice, Muckross, Harnane, Castle Lough and other lands were restored to Dame Sarah Mac-Carthy, daughter of the Earl of Antrim and widow of Daniel MacCarthy Mór. The second son of Dame Sarah, Florence, sold Cahirnane Castle and lands to Maurice Hussey in 1684 and gave Castle Lough to his cousin Denis MacCarthy.

Castle MacEllistrim
Parish: Tralee: Traighlí—strand of Lee river
Townland: Balloonagh

This castle is situated to the north of the town, a little west of Rockstreet and on the north side of Balloonagh townland, which was a short distance from the Great Castle and the Short Castle.

It was built of limestone with lime and sand mortar and was grouted. The building stood on low but level ground in the north of Balloonagh townland.

In the Ordnance Survey letters of 1841, O'Donovan describes the remains as consisting of the ground floor up to the height of an arch which had carried the floor above. The ground area covered was only about 30 square feet and there was a spiral stairway in a corner tower. This stairway gave access to the different storeys of the main building. O'Donovan also describes a number of windows and a pointed doorway of chiselled limestone at the south-east corner and it would seem that this was a small tower house rather than a fortress.

Historical references are almost entirely lacking. There is a tradition that it dated from around 1450 and was the seat of an Anglo-Norman family called Fitzalexander, who were important tenants of the Desmonds. There is record of a grant of £10 being given in that year by the Crown for the fortification of a house. The Fitzalexanders later changed their name to MacEllistrim. The tower house was largely destroyed in the Elizabethan war around 1580. Whatever vestiges of the castle remained were occupied by a Christopher Walsh in 1641. No references to this castle appear in the events of the Siege of Tralee.

Castlemaine Castle
Caislean Cois Mainge
Parish: Kilcolman: Cill Cholmáin—church of St Colman
Townland: Castlemaine: Caisleán na Mainge—castle of the river Maine
O.S. map 71 ref 835 030

This castle was erected c. 1215 and was supposed to have been built by Maurice, son of Thomas Fitzgerald, to command the crossing of the river Maine, but others say that it was built jointly by the Earl of Desmond and the MacCarthy Mórs and that they agreed to fortify it in turns. This was the dividing line between the territories of the Desmonds and the MacCarthys.

When the MacCarthys handed over the castle to the Earl of Desmond, the latter refused to hand it back at the end of the agreed period. The Fitzgeralds continued to hold the castle up to the time of Elizabeth I.

From the engraving in *Pacata Hibernia*, it can be seen that it was an unusual castle, standing on a bridge of four arches rising to three floors. In 1600 it had a tower with a flat roof and battlements. In addition, it had another tower with a plain gable roof, a portcullis, windows, strong walls and possibly a drawbridge at one end. The castle stood on and over the bridge and projected considerably on the east side, supported by an arch, the buttress of which could still be seen in the 1830s, as could the stone socket in which the pivot of the castle gates turned. Both the Desmond and the Cromwellian forces realised its importance, as it was almost impregnable.

In 1357, Maurice Óg, second son of Thomas Fitzgerald, died in the castle. In 1510, the Lord Deputy, Gerald, Earl of Kildare, captured the castle but on his retreat to Limerick he was defeated by the Munster forces of Desmond and

CASTLEMAGNE.

Thomond. Later, the Earl of Kildare together with his five uncles were executed at Tyburn.

Ten years later in 1567, the Earl of Desmond and his brother, Sir John Desmond, were arrested and taken to the Tower of London. Meanwhile, Sir John Perrott, as Lord President in 1570, destroyed every castle in Munster that had not surrendered to his forces by the end of 1571. James Fitzmaurice Fitzgerald, together with MacCarthy Mór, gained the castle and placed a defence force to hold the castle against Perrott and his army. Perrott was half brother to Queen Elizabeth. Eventually, when Perrott took the castle, the garrison were released as free men.

Earlier in July 1571, the then Lord President of Munster wrote to the Lord Chief Justices in Dublin stating that Castlemaine should be taken. A month earlier in the same year, Fitzwilliam commenced a siege but, due to lack of gunpowder and cannon, he was forced to give up. In June of the following year, the siege was renewed and continued into August. Eventually the garrison yielded and Perrott, who was now in charge, made John Herbert the constable of the castle. John Herbert took over the castle with ten men on 10 November 1572. The Earl of Desmond put in his garrison on 24 December 1573 and gave the keys to Captain William Apsley. John Herbert was killed in 1579 along with forty English and a hundred foot soldiers when they sallied forth from the castle. He was succeeded by Andrew Martyn and, in 1583, Captain Cheston took over. Later, in 1586, the castle was held by Thomas Spring of Lavenham in Suffolk, with a lieutenant and sixteen privates.

Queen Elizabeth sent a gown of gold cloth to Elinor, Countess of Desmond, as a sign of affection, hoping that she might bring peace to Munster. Before the gown was dispatched to Elinor it was examined in Dublin and found to be 'slobbered' and stained (i.e., second-hand). Before the gown finally arrived, Elinor was busy trying to hold on to her husband's lands while he was imprisoned in London. She was looked on by the English as a means of getting peace due to her influence over the other chieftains in Munster. Queen Elizabeth favoured the Earl of Desmond, much to the displeasure of her advisers, including Sir Valentine Brown and other undertakers in the province of Munster.

A letter of 1583 from Ormond to Burleigh stated that Donnell MacDonnell O'Moriarty, who dwelt near Castlemaine, had slain the Earl of Desmond. This was probably O'Moriarty of Castle Drum. Moriarty was constable of the MacCarthy Mór at that time and foster-father of Ellen MacCarthy, the heiress to the title of Clancarre and its estates. Both the O'Moriarty brothers were hunted down and captured alive. One was hanged in England and the other at Clanmaurice Castle by the Lord of Lixnaw.

It is reported that John MacUlick, who was in possession of O'Brennan's Castle at that time, and James Fitzdavid were aiding the old Earl of Desmond in Glaungentha when he was attacked by the O'Kellys and the Moriartys, who happened to be his foster-brothers, while a Cornelius O'Daly was looking after their few cattle some distance away. When Ormond was informed that the Earl had been killed, he ordered that Desmond's body be taken to Cork and hung in chains. However, the headless corpse was moved from place to place by some of his loyal followers.

One of the stories about the rebel Earl of Desmond, who also had two other castles near Lough Gur, was that he was not really dead but was forced to live under the murky waters of the nearby lake by a magic spell. Once in very seven years, on a certain date, he was supposed to rise at midnight and ride around the lake on a white horse visiting his castles and then return to the depths of the lake, where he was said to live in another castle.

After a long captivity in London, the Earl of Desmond was allowed to return to Dublin, but in 1573 he escaped and began his journey to his Palatinate. He was at once proclaimed a traitor and a reward was posted—a thousand pounds if captured alive and five hundred for his head.

In 1612, Sir Nicholas Brown got possession of Cois Mainge, Molahiffe and the castle at Molan.

Nothing remains today of Castlemaine Castle.

Castle Quin

Parish: Caher/Cahirciveen: Cathair Saidhbhín—little stone fort of Sadhbh (Sabina)
Townland: Garranebane/Garranebawn
Location: west of present-day Cahirciveen town

This is believed to have been a castle of the O'Mahony clan. Another reference gives its location as south of the Valencia river in Garranebawn townland.

It was described as a small castle or watchtower. This site was later occupied by a bungalow. There is also mention in some of the old records of a castle called Srugreena. This townland is about 5 kilometres east of Cahirciveen.

See Short Castle 1.

These two castles are both indicated on the 1756 map in Smith's *History of County Kerry*.

Castle Shannon
Clochan Seanain
Parish: Killury/Killoory: Cill Luraigh—church of St Lurach
Townland: Castleshannon

No traces of the castle exist today and it is almost impossible to give its exact location.
According to Smith (1756) the castle was at one time occupied by Rev. Thomas Connor, the cantor of Ardfert Monastery. It was located in the same area as Ballingarry and west of Mineghane.

Cloghane Castle
Parish: Cloghane: Clothain—stone-roofed house
Townland: Cloghane

This castle was believed to have been situated in Cloghane parish, north of Ventry. There is a Cloghane townland, also a Ballinahow townland. Nothing else is known about it.

Clonmellane Castle
Cluain Maolain Castle
Parish: Kilnanare: Cill na Aen
Townland: Clonmellane
2.5 kilometres north-west of Fieries
O.S. map 71 ref 889 042

This was a stone castle built by the Geraldines *c.* 1217. The castles of Molahiffe and Fieries are within a very short distance of each other, along the river Maine. It is said that the three castles were connected to each other by tunnels. The castle was built on a round hillock close to the river Maine. Little remains except for a piece of the north-west corner. It seems that the walls were over 9 feet thick.

After the Geraldine defeat at the Battle of Callan in 1261, the family of Owen Mór MacCarthy of Cois Mainge held these castles until 1583 when they were forfeited after the Geraldine confiscations. Cormac MacCarthy held the three castles. Following the Battle of Kinsale in 1601, a Charles Herbert was in residence at Clonmellane.

The three castles were later taken over by Sir Valentine Brown. The Browns married O'Sullivan, MacCarthy and Fitzgerald wives and became one of the chief Catholic peerages. They were MacCarthy castles and by 1837, together with their lands, they belonged to the Earls of Kenmare.

Currans Castle

Parish: Currans: Na Corrain—small round hill
Townland: Meanus
Location: close to the confluence of the Maine and Brown Flesk rivers about 2 kilometres north of Farranfore

Very little is known about this castle. It was one of a line of thirteenth-century Norman castles on the river Maine, which was the border between old Kerry and Desmond. It is not mentioned in later years.

Presumably, it was destroyed or deteriorated and was never replaced with a later structure. It is possible that it was never a stone structure at all but some sort of fortification, but this is speculative. An early eighteenth-century Currans House existed on or near the site, which has also completely disappeared.

Derryquin Castle

Parish: Kilcrohane: Cill Crócháin—church of St Crochan
Townland: Derryquin

There is some doubt as to whether a castle called Derryquin ever existed. No written records can be found today. Yet, local folklore indicates that there was an ancient castle on or near the site of the later castellated mansion of the Bland family, which was sometimes referred to as Castle Quin. This building is mentioned in 1772.

If it did exist, it probably would have been owned by O'Sullivan Mór, as it is located on his territory.

The castellated mansion of the Blands, and later of a Colonel Warden, was burned almost to the ground in 1922.

Dingle Castle

Daingean de Cousa or Dain-gean-ni-Cushy, Dingle-I-Couch—
Fortress or Castle of Hussey
Dingle: Daingean Uí Chuis: O'Cuis: Hussey.

In 1756, the vaults of the original Hussey Castle were being used as the town gaol. Some walls still stood in the nineteenth century when there was a cobbler's shop within the thickness of one wall.

There were three castles in the Dingle area:

No. 1: Dingle Castle
Hussey's Castle/Earl of Desmond
Location: in the town of Dingle and reputed to have been the first castle built in Dingle

This castle was built by the Husseys, who were barons from County Meath and probably a family of the early Anglo-Normans who came to Ireland. Later it was forfeited by the Earl of Desmond as well as Castlegregory, Ballinahow, etc., and granted to the Earl of Ormond after the rebellion.

It was later bought, with adjoining lands, by Fitzgerald, the Knight of Kerry, who by this time had his own castle in the town. In 1600, the 'Sugán Earl' of Desmond fired the town and the Knight of Kerry gave up the castle to Sir Charles Wilmot. Smith refers to the castle and how the vaults became the gaol of Dingle. The site of Hussey's Castle is said to have been located behind the market house in the 1840s. Nothing remains of the castle today. Walter Hussey lost his life in the heroic defence of Minard Castle.

A detailed account of the Hussey family can be found in The *Old Kerry Records* (1872) by Mary Hickson.

The Treaty of Dingle

One of the most important diplomatic events to take place in Ireland during the sixteenth century was the Treaty of Dingle. Signed on 28 April 1529, between James Fitzgerald, eleventh Earl of Desmond, and the Holy Roman Emperor of the German nation and King of Spain, Charles V, it granted the Irish the rights and privileges of citizenship within the domains of the Habsburg Empire. It was signed in such a format that the Geraldines could consolidate their position, secure their borders and strengthen their economy within their palatinate in south Munster, which was then like a mini-state within Ireland. Broadly speaking, it could be described as the blueprint for the EU. In addition to its diplomatic involvement, it gave the Irish the same rights as the Spaniards in Spain in respect of obtaining office or employment, while all other foreigners were barred. In Spain at that time, the Irish were regarded as 'northern Spaniards' or *'los Españoles del norte'*.

While the emperor valued an alliance with Desmond, he did not want to upset his cousin, Queen Mary Tudor; Desmond would have to be accommodated in any Anglo-Imperial treaty but without Charles V assuming the overlordship of the palatinate. On 16 October 1529, the envoy of James Fitzgerald, Sherek, arrived in San Sebastian and made his way to the imperial court at Toledo bearing gifts and a pair of Irish hawks and wolfhounds. This was considered an affront to the English monarch, who had claimed the rights to all falcons and hawks in Ireland.

Secretly, the King sent his envoy from Toledo in March 1529. The imperial envoy, Fernandez, eventually sailed into Bearehaven, the seat of O'Sullivan Bere, and stayed at Dunboy Castle. Letters were sent to and from the Earl of Desmond and, on 21 April, Fernandez was received with full honours by James Fitzgerald, his council, the corporation and the people of Dingle. He was fêted at Desmond Castle and presented the Earl with a 'love cup' as a sign of friendship from the Emperor.

After a week's negotiations, the treaty—in the form of *supplicatio* (supplication)—was signed and sealed. In it Desmond stated his submission to the imperial authority of Charles V, hoping that the King would protect a lesser prince from the English monarchy. All that can be said at this time is that this was just wishful thinking, as the relationship between Spain and England deteriorated quickly, later culminating in declaration of war and the dispatch of the Spanish Armada to invade England. Meanwhile, the Desmonds went into rebellion and lost their high position in early Irish politics as well as most of their lands, notwithstanding the arrival of the Spanish/Italian force at Smerwick harbour.

Dingle was the only town in the barony in 1585. Queen Elizabeth incorporated it and gave it a charter that same year, as well as a grant of £300 to build a wall around the town.

No. 2: Knights of Kerry Castle

Fitzgerald also had another old castle in the town, which was said to have been a substantial tower house with large gardens.

Regrettably, we can find no details, if they exist, of the structure at this time, but it is reputed to have been a very large castle with twin towers and a bawn of some considerable size. It is said to have been erected in 1580 but this date seems very late. Dingle was described in 1574 as 'a substantial stronghold with large towers at each end', which may correspond with Hussey's Castle and that of the Knight of Kerry.

No. 3: Rice Castle

This castle was located near to Dingle (see Burnham Castle, earlier called Ballingoleen) and existed before the wars of 1641. Piers Rice built a castle or fortification at Smerwick on an outcrop of rock. James Desmond later cut a piece out of the rock, measuring about 40 feet in length, about 20 feet broad and 20 feet deep, to make its position stronger. It was later referred to as the 'Island of Ardcanny' or the fort of Swerwick harbour. After the Cromwellian forfeitures, the Rice family, in the Barony of Corcaguiny, lost almost all their lands.

The old Catholic presbytery, formally Rice House, was recently changed into offices and still exists. It is not known for certain if this was the original Rice House or a part of it, yet it is a substantial building. Smith refers to a house in 1756 with a marble doorway, window surrounds and a plaque dating 1563. Some time later, it came into the possession of Count James Louis Rice, who was an officer in the Irish Brigade in France. Being a regular guest at the royal palace in France, he became infatuated with Marie Antoinette, and when she was imprisoned in the Bastille he arranged to secure her escape and bring her to live in his house in Dingle. The house had been completely renovated in the French style at great cost to accommodate a person of her standing. The plan for her escape was foolproof. He was to visit her with his 'wife'—a prostitute, who was terminally ill—who agreed to change places for a small sum of gold. The woman was dressed up in royal garments and accompanied the Count to the cell. After much argument, Marie Antoinette declined the offer to escape and remained in her cell. She refused to desert her husband, children and France for a foreign country and eventually ended up under the guillotine.

Some say that the house was haunted by a man dressed in the apparel of that time, with sword, dagger and high boots. At the present time, there are no records of where and when Count Rice died.

It is interesting to note that, up to that time, Dingle was recognised as a Spanish town. The old houses were all built with balconies in the Spanish fashion and the church was dedicated to St James of Santiago. It was estimated that almost half the population of the old town were Spanish merchants and tradesmen and their families had all the usual characteristics of straight black hair, dark eyes and swarthy complexion. The women wore the Galician traditional dress with tight buttoned bodices and layers of petticoats and their black embroidered mantillas.

Note: Richard Boyle purchased the Barony of Corcaguiny in 1611. He was a student at the Middle Temple in London and came to Ireland seeking his fortune. He arrived in Cork with £27 in his pocket, his sword and his favourite dagger.

It is difficult to understand that in 1616 he was Lord Boyle and in 1631 he was Earl of Cork.

Doon Castle
An Dun Thoir—The Devil's Castle
Parish: Kilconly: Cill Chonnla—church of St Connla
Townland: Kilconly
O.S. map 63 ref 864 433
Also referred to as Dune or Deune Castle

Doon or Dune Castle probably gets its name from a rock off the coastline, which was called Caislean an Deamain or the Devil's Castle and was situated north of Ballybunion and Pookeenee, at Doon Point, northwest of Doon RC church.

The castle was built on the edge of a precipice by the MacCarthys after their arrival in Kerry, according to some sources. However, it is more likely that it was built some time after 1220 to hamper the invasion of the Anglo-Normans along the coastline. Very little remains of the castle, which was probably a watchtower, except fragments of walls. Most of the stone was removed over the centuries for the building of houses nearby. It was reputed to have been a substantial castle which was taken over by the Fitzgeralds, who were extremely cruel in their time.

It would be interesting to discover how it got the name Devil's Castle. Perhaps it was renowned in the olden days for its atrocities.

Drum Castle
Castledrum—Castle Dromin
Parish: Kilgarrylander: Cill Gharraidh Londrais—church of Garrylander
Townland: Castle Dromin
Location: 3 kilometres west of Castlemaine
O.S. map 71 ref 790 030

The castle was situated some distance east of the old church, south of White Gate crossroads. Nothing remains now except a heap of rubble.

In 1641–2, one of the Irish rebels besieging Tralee was Captain Donnell McMoriarty of Castle Drum. It was later taken by the Cromwellian forces and handed over to one of the Moriartys. The castle was destroyed in 1641 and demolished in 1652.

There are two Ogham stones in the immediate vicinity.

In Desmond West Cork

Dunamark Castle
Dun na Mbarc—fortress of the ships
Parish: Kilmacomogue—church of young St Colman
Townland: Dunamark
Location: 2.5 kilometres north of Bantry centre

All that can be seen now of Dunamark Castle are some loose stones scattered over the original site. It is shown on maps as a rectangular tower house, maybe of three or four storeys, on an isthmus jutting out into Bantry harbour. It was reputed to have been built in 1215 by the Norman knight, Robert Carew, who was a cousin of the Fitzgeralds and the Fitzthomases, who came over to Ireland before Strongbow. The Carews were styled the Marquises of Cork and built various castles along the coast. Dunamark itself is mentioned in the *Irish Annals* as being the location where Cesair, the first person to set foot in Ireland, landed after the Flood with her retenue of fifty warrior maidens and three surviving young men. When the women were divided amongst the three men, one is said to have died from a surfeit of sex.

When Diarmuid MacCarthy of south Munster submitted to Henry II, he created division and upheaval within the ranks of his clan and the junior MacCarthy septs. He was kidnapped and held prisoner by his own son. While the ensuing interclan struggle was raging, Normans such as Carew were busy strengthening their position in West Cork. It is said that Dunamark was one of the earliest Norman castles in Munster.

Around 1260, Finghin MacCarthy's cousin, Eoin Ó Muircheartaigh, was killed by the Carews, and in revenge

Finghin gathered a powerful force to storm and destroy the Carew castles in West Cork, including Dunamark, on his way to Callan, where he was to await the advancing Anglo-Norman forces. Dunamark Castle was razed to the ground, like the other Carew castles. Later the castles and adjoining lands were in the possession of Owen O'Sullivan Jr and his descendants, who, with the help of the Crown, repelled various claims on the castle and lands by individuals purporting to be relatives of Richard Carew.

Almost all of the stones and building materials of the castle were used in later years for the construction of the mills and brewery of the Murphy family at Dunamark.

In Desmond West Cork

Dunboy Castle

Parish: Kilaconenagh: Cill Acha n'Aoineach—church of St Acha of the fastings
Townland: Dunboy: Dunbaoi—Baoi's fort
O.S. map 84 ref 668 440

The original territory of the O'Driscolls extended from the Bandon river to Dursey Island off the tip of the Beara peninsula, which was called Oilean Baei Bheirre. They were the most powerful overlords in West Cork up to the Anglo-Norman invasion, although their power had been fading since the arrival of the displaced tribes of north Munster, which included the O'Mahonys and the O'Donovans, amongst others. One of their most western outposts was a fortified timber enclosure surrounded by sea, fossa and a moat called Dun Baoi. It was on this particular site that Dermod O'Sullivan built his stone castle.

Dunboy was a rectangular tower house, with an adjoining

square tower and large bawn. The main section measured about 13 by 17 metres and had a large entertainment hall and upper accommodation. It probably had the best long hall for entertainment in all of West Cork and Kerry.

The entrance was at the far end of the west wall, and a straight mural stairway ascended to the first floor. Later, a smaller bawn or courtyard was built as an extension to the east of the main building *c.* AD 1600.

No exact date is given for the building of the castle, but the best indications from the available records suggest that it was around 1473 when Dermod, with his wife Sheela, moved out of Castledermot, finding it too small for their large family. His wife Sheela was a daughter of Donal MacCarthy Reagh, to whom he had pledged allegiance. His son Donal should have inherited the chieftainship from him but his brother Owen succeeded in obtaining the position, as Donal was too young and still a minor at school in Wexford. He later turned out to be a wild young man, spending his time with his paternal grandmother at Rosmacowen.

Only when the position of chieftainship and the division of the O'Sullivan territory were settled did he return to Dunboy and Sir Owen move out. Probably around this time he married Ellen, a daughter of Donnell O'Brien of Thomond. There is some uncertainty about this union, as in later reports his wife is mentioned as a daughter of Owen O'Sullivan of Desmond, who was also called Ellen. Now, supported by his uncles, Dermod of Dursey and Philip of Ardea Castle, he became more adventurous and ventured east to Bantry. Finding the Franciscan abbey in the hands of Captain Zouch (later noted for the massacre of Smerwick) and a large garrison, he attacked. Taken by surprise, the English force was defeated and fled back to Cork.

When informed that the Spaniards under Don Zubiaur had arrived in Castlehaven in 1601, Donal declared allegiance to the Spanish king and immediately marched to Castlehaven in twenty-four hours with over five hundred men. Finding the Spaniards under severe attack from the English, he immediately went into action and saved the situation. Later, he joined O'Neill and O'Donnell at Kinsale with the other West Cork and Kerry troops. After the defeat of the Irish forces, Donal retreated back to Dunboy and immediately set about fortifying his castle. Unable to force a way by land to Dunboy, Carew finally transported his army by sea to Castletown and, having taken Castledermot, laid siege to Dunboy, which was taken with much bloodshed on 18 June 1602. Carew ordered that the castle be completely destroyed. Some years later, a star-shaped fortification was erected on the site, yet some parts of the original walls still exist today.

Dunkerron Castle
Caislean Duna Ciarain, Caislean Dune Inse an Duaine, Caislean Duin Mic Temain
Parish: Templenoe: Teampall Nuadh—new temple
Townland: Dunkerron: Dun Ciarain—fort of Ciaran
Location: 3 kilometres west-south-west of Kenmare in the grounds of Dunkerron house
O.S. map 78 ref 884 705

The castle was built on a high rock. Even though it was in ruins in 1841, the north wall where it was joined to the east wall stood over 60 feet tall. The remainder was in ruins. There are indications that there was an arch inside the north wall. It appears that the castle contained four floors—two floors under the arch and two more above it. The doorway was situated on the south wall. The dimensions were 48 feet by 45 feet, while the thickness

Dunkerron Castle

of the wall was over 8 feet. It was a narrow peel house or caslet and was also referred to as the Court of Dunkerron and reputed to have been built by Owen O'Sullivan Mór and his wife Calia MacCarthy.

Dunkerron was reputed to have been built by Carew c. 1215 on a pre-existing fort. Some time around 1450 it was rebuilt by a grandson of Roderick O'Sullivan Mór and later became the main seat of the O'Sullivan Mórs after the castle had fallen into English hands in 1595. It became the property of O'Sullivan Mór c. 1261. The castle was rebuilt in the fifteenth century and added to in 1596. It was burnt in 1646 to avoid being captured by the Cromwellian forces.

In 1580, Owen O'Sullivan became O'Sullivan Mór and he and his second wife, Sily Ny Donagh MacCarthy Reagh of County Cork, are said to have built a manor house adjoining the castle. This Sily, Celia or Sheila, was the sister of Florence MacCarthy Reagh, who was held prisoner in the Tower of London.

The castle was burnt by Lord Muskerry to prevent it being taken over by the advancing Cromwellian forces. A Taylor family built a house near the castle and were in occupation there at least before 1712.

It continued to be the residence of O'Sullivan Mór until 1656, when it was confiscated and passed to Sir William Petty and to the Marquis of Lansdowne. The barony consists of the parishes of Kilcrohane, Templenoe Kinchane and part of Killorglin. There is a story that when one O'Sullivan Mór, the last of his direct line, died in 1762, he left many books and manuscripts. It later transpired that his great-grandson burned a heap of ancient manuscripts, including some written on hides in Latin and old Irish. It is fascinating to imagine what these might have contained.

A stone was found near the castle ruins bearing the arms of O'Sullivan Mór and the following inscription:

'I.H.S. Maria deo gratias. This work was made the xx apreill 1596 by Owen O'Sullivan Mór and Sily Ny Donagh MacCarthy Riogh.'

A picture and further information about stones can be found in the *Archaeological Survey of South Kerry*.

To the south-east of the castle ruins is the wall of a large house with a chimney.

As a point of interest, Abainn Chinnmara was the ancient name for Kenmare river.

Dunloe Castle
Caislean an Dun Loith
Dún Lóich—fort of the river Loe
Parish: Knockaun: Cnochain—hillock
Townland: Dunloe lower
O.S. map 78 ref 884 913

Dunloe Castle is situated on the edge of a cliff overlooking the river Laune, which takes the water from the lakes of Killarney to the sea. It was probably built to command the river crossing and the pass through the Gap of Dunloe. Dunloe was originally an old-style fortress and, when the Normans recognised its unique position, they built a castle at the location.

According to the *Annals,* the original structure was built by Maurice, son of Thomas Fitzgerald, in the year 1215. Earlier a fortification had been granted to a Fitzphilip in 1207. Afterwards it became the seat of the Donal O'Sullivan Mór following the Battle of Callan in 1261. The original structure was probably destroyed around 1280. The tower house that replaced it was associated with the O'Sullivan Mórs and became prominent during the Desmond rebellion.

DUNLOE

During the Elizabethan wars it was almost destroyed by the Duke of Ormond but was reoccupied by the O'Sullivans, one of whom, Daniel, represented Kerry in parliament in 1613. Later, it was badly damaged by Ludlow on his way to attack Ross Castle. The castle was forfeited in 1656 and acquired by William Petty. Late in the seventeenth century, it was in the hands of the O'Mahony family, who still owned it in the 1820s, when one of them altered and restored it.

It is located about 7 miles from Killarney at the west end of the lake. The floors are of fine yew planks, a wood that, if well worked, has a more beautiful grain and polish than mahogany. In fact, it had only one room per floor as far as can be ascertained. It can be described as a watchtower castle due to its size.

Many stories are told about Daniel O'Mahony, who inherited the castle *c.* 1705. He ruled south Kerry with a strong hand for over forty years. On his deathbed, he bequeathed his velvet breeches and sword to his favourite daughter, saying that she was the only person fit to have them and rule his dominion like a man. The O'Mahonys were still in possession of the castle in 1750.

In 1841, all that was left was the keep and a slender square tower.

In Desmond West Cork

Dursey Castle
Oileann Beag Castle
Doirse: Gates—Thor Iy: Island of Thor (Norse god of war)
O.S. map 84 ref 505 410

The name of the island is open to various interpretations. It could refer to the gates of Hades, as the cave on the nearby Bull Rock was, according to ancient legend, the entrance to Hades. It is more likely that it was called Thor Iy because the Vikings used the island as a raiding base for centuries.

This O'Sullivan castle was actually situated on Oilean Beag (small island) and was known as Dursey Castle because of its location at the southernmost tip of the section nearest Dursey Island. Surrounded by sea and cliffs on the south, east and west sides and on raised ground on the north, its defensive potential was great. Indeed, the castle's purpose was purely defensive, and not residential at all. Access was difficult, and there was no well or spring, the nearest water supply being a spring located near the drawbridge to Dursey Island.

The fortification itself was divided into three sections. The main section included the castle and a watchtower, whose walls were over a metre thick. In the middle was a rectangular enclosure measuring about 30 by 23 metres, which housed the gardens and a few storage buildings. To the south was an almost triangular section, which was probably used as an animal enclosure.

Dermod O'Sullivan (An Phdair, The Powder) is reputed to have built this castle. It was occupied by another Dermod, uncle of Donal Cam O'Sullivan, in the middle of the seventeenth century. Dermod was an old man when he joined the epic march to Leitrim. He was married to a Joanna MacSweeney and they had eighteen children.

While Dunboy was besieged, three Spanish cannons and Conor O'Driscoll with forty men were sent to the defence of Dursey. While the guns were being placed and the castle fortified, Carew organised roughly one hundred and forty soldiers, under the command of Captain John Bostock and a Lieutenant Downing, to go by sea at night and take Dursey Castle. When Sir Owen O'Sullivan of Carriganass offered to take his own troops along, Carew did not object. Sir Owen had his reasons for participating, not least that his wife had been placed for safety in Dursey Castle by Donal Cam.

The soldiers landed on the island at dawn and, as one of the ships bombarded the castle with cannon fire, the soldiers began to fire at those on the defences. Soon those inside surrendered and the castle was taken.

The surviving defenders were taken by ship to Castletown, as well as Owen's wife, who was found hiding in a barrel in the cellar. On the penultimate day of the siege of Dunboy, the prisoners were marched before the walls and hanged, which is likely to have convinced those inside the walls to die fighting.

Even though Philip O'Sullivan, the historian, states that all the people of Dursey were massacred at this time, other sources state that the massacre took place some months later when Wilmot, in command of the English forces, laid bare the peninsula and took his vengeance on the people still living on Dursey. Descriptions of the atrocities committed differ, but the unspeakable horror of the slaughter darkened the history of the English forces in Ireland. Men, women and children were rounded up and shot, hacked to death or run through with swords. Pregnant women had their bellies slit and the unborn were paraded around on the end of spears.

Those remaining alive or injured were tied back to back and pushed over the cliff to their deaths. A few survived hidden in a cave on the cliff face to tell the tale.

A point worth mentioning is that, when the English army was on its way back to Bantry, the weather deteriorated rapidly with severe snow storms and icy conditions. It became so bad that gun carriages and baggage carts had to be abandoned. It is said that over fifteen hundred soldiers perished. The Lord took his own revenge for the murder of the innocents.

Fenit Castle

Parish: Fenit: Fianaid
Townland: Fenit
Location: about 12 kilometres north-west of Tralee, guarding the harbour entrance
Referred to as Fianainn Castle by the *Four Masters*
O.S. map 71 ref 723 179

The castle was situated at the north-east end of Fenit Island on a rock which is separated from the island itself, except for a narrow neck of land, and was surrounded by the sea on all sides. It is now in ruins. It stood on the shore of the Barrow inlet about 60 feet high and the walls were over 7 feet thick.

Measuring 29 feet by 33 feet, it was clearly a substantial castle. Part of the south wall adjoining the west wall can be seen. The west and north wall retain most of their original height.

This castle was built by the Fitzmaurices to protect the harbour from pirates and was almost completely destroyed in 1641. There are a few references to a MacMorris family as well a Sir John Locke, a Cromwellian planter, who lived in the vicinity of the castle.

Barrow harbour was guarded by three castles: Tawlought, which has disappeared, the tower house at Fenit and the round tower of Barrow.

Ferriter's Castle
Dunorlan Castle or Castle Sybil
Parish: Dunorlan: Dun Urlann—Dunurlin
Townland: Ballyoughteragh
O.S. map 70 ref 322 054

The Ferriter family (Le Fureter) settled in and around Dingle. Their castle, which stood on a rocky promontory fort called Doon Point, was built c. 1460. The castle is situated about a quarter of a mile from the old church ruins. It was surrounded by sea on all sides, except for a narrow piece of land about 60 feet wide. The castle was built of green stone (probably copper based) and red and brown sandstone. It is estimated that the castle stood over 55 feet high and got narrower towards the top.

Situated between Ballyferriter and Sybil Head, the ruins stand on an isthmus of land surrounded by the sea on the north, south and west. The castle was protected by a deep trench on the land side. It had a stone arch and a spiral stairway which ran up the tower in the south-west corner, while the doorway was on the west wall. It is sometimes referred to as Castle Sybil or otherwise Elizabeth's Castle. It is said to have been built by a widow of one of the Ferriters.

The name of Castle Sybil is derived from the tragic story of a lady called Sybil Lynch from Galway. It seems that, when one of the Ferriters went to Galway, he encountered this young woman and she fell in love with him and accompanied him back to Kerry. When her enraged father came looking for her, she was hidden in one of the caves beneath the castle and was drowned by the rising tide.

One of the inhabitants during the early seventeenth century was Pierce Ferriter, a renowned poet, scholar and author. In 1641, Lady Kerry wrote to him advising him not to join the insurrection. He never received the letter. Later, he was one of the chief besiegers of Tralee Castle and, when he was eventually captured, he was hanged in 1653, on the orders of Brigadier Nelson, along with Pierce Moriarty, O'Connor Kerry and many other leaders, at a place called Chnocain na gCaorach near Killarney. Many of those taken prisoner were transported to Jamaica, probably out of Cork harbour. All Ferriter's lands and the castle were forfeited.

When Pierce Ferriter found himself on the run and hiding from the English, he crossed over to the Great Blasket seeking refuge and spent some time in a house in the small village. When the English became aware of his whereabouts, the troops landed unnoticed early one morning. The house where he was staying was immediately surrounded. Knowing that there was no means of escape, Pierce went to the door and surrendered. He then invited the soldiers in out of the cold and rain for something to eat and drink. While they drank poteen and became a bit intoxicated, the woman of the house managed to pour water into their muskets. When the time came to leave, Pierce made a run for it and when the soldiers aimed their guns and pulled the triggers nothing happened. Lucky to have escaped, Pierce quickly made his way to an almost inaccessible cave in the cliff on the south side of the island. Thinking that he had fallen to his death, the soldiers departed from the island. Pierce remained on the island for another few weeks and eventually made his way to

Dingle, where he was recognised by a spy and captured and taken to Killarney.

There are many tales of mermaids being seen around the location of the castle. There were various sightings of them returning to the beaches to collect the skins that they had shed during the late summer months.

In the context of this castle, some mention must be made concerning the massacre at Smerwick Fort. This was against all codes of battle at this period of time, as a white flag had been displayed and a surrender had been accepted. This was regarded in Europe as the code of practice during warfare but did not seem to apply in Ireland for the period 1200 to 1723. Over six hundred, including four hundred Italians, Spanish, Irish and women and children, were executed.

Captain John Zouch was in command of part of the English forces, which consisted of four hundred foot soldiers, fifty horses and some small cannons. Most of his force died of cholera shortly after in Dingle. Later, when reinforcements arrived, he raided Aghadoe Castle in 1581. He hanged the Baron of Lixnaw at Ardfert. When he returned to England he was killed in a duel.

Frederick Champion took possession of the castle in 1584, as well as Castlemaine Castle and the Blasket Island. These were later purchased by Sir Richard Boyle of Cork.

Fermoyle Castle

Parish: Prior: Paraiste an Phriora—parish of the prior
Townland: Fermoyle: Formaoil
Location: about 6 kilometres from Ballinskelligs
O.S. map 83 ref 453 706

This castle was in ruins at the beginning of the nineteenth century. It measured about 27 feet by 25 feet and the walls were about 6 feet thick. At the south-east corner was a guards' room with a stone roof and the spiral stairway was situated nearby. This guards' room measured about 9 feet by about 8 feet. There were no visible remains by the 1840s. Much of the original stone is said to have gone into the building of Fermoyle House and other local buildings.

It is reputed that the castle was built by the Fermoyle family, who were related to O'Sullivan Mór. The O'Sullivans of Fermoyle and Ballycarna are given as a sub-sept of the O'Sullivan Mórs. (See O'Donovan, p. 176.)

See also Ballycarna Castle in the parish of Kilcrohane.

Captain Owen O'Sullivan received serious injuries nearby at the Battle of Ballinskelligs.

Fieries Castle
Foighre Castle
Parish: Kilnanane: Cill na nAen—church of stone builders
Townland: Fieries: Na Foidhrí—wooded land
Location: about 1 kilometre south of Fieries
O.S. map 71 ref 906 024

The castle stands on a high rock in the valley and seems to have had twin towers, possibly something like Listowel Castle. The east tower is completely destroyed and the other remains about 10 feet high and measures about 38 by 35 feet, with walls 7 feet thick built of large blocks of limestone. The first floor rested on an arch. The south-east corner is about all that remains of this castle, which originally stood on raised ground on a plain. It appears that it was built of large blocks of limestone with walls over 9 feet thick and possibly up to 60 feet in height.

Probably built *c.* 1217 by Thomas Fitzmaurice, First Lord of Kerry, who obtained a grant for the surrounding lands from King John. It seems that, shortly after the castle was built, he gave the Moriartys a lease on the castle and lands. They happened to be the original owners of the lands. The second Lord of Kerry, Maurice Fitzthomas Fitzmaurice, died in the castle in 1306. Following the Battle of Callan in 1261, the O'Donoghues of the Glens took possession, but the MacCarthy Mórs of Coshmange gained possession some time later.

The Coshmange—a tribe of the river Maine—held the borders between the MacCarthys and the Fitzgeralds, which extended from Castlemaine to the Cork border. Together with the castles of Molahiffe and Clonmellane, they presented the dividing line. In time, three branches of the O'Donoghues took over the defences, each residing in separate castles. When the Desmond wars commenced, the

O'Donoghues pledged their allegiance to Desmond, which brought them into direct conflict with their overlords, the MacCarthys, and the English forces, which later resulted in the death at Aghadoe Castle of the chief of the O'Donoghues, namely Teige MacDermod MacCormac (O'Donoghue). After the war, all the lands of the O'Donoghues were confiscated by the Crown and were given to the Brown family. The MacCarthys successfully claimed this land back under Queen Elizabeth. MacCarthy then remortgaged his old lands to the Browns. After this, most of the tribe of O'Donoghue left Ireland for France.

Fieries Castle later passed to the O'Connor family as a marriage gift from MacCarthy Mór. O'Connors lived at Fieries at least until 1833. The castle does not appear to have been attacked by Cromwell's forces when the other Coshmange castles at Clonmellane and Molahiffe were subdued. This may have been because of its association with the MacCarthy Mórs. The O'Connors of Fieries, although originally a sub-branch of the Carrigafoyle family, later became known as 'The O'Connor Kerrys'.

Molahiffe, Fieries and Clonmellane were all on the banks of the river Maine. They were originally all MacCarthy castles but, by 1837, belonged to the Earls of Kenmare.

Gallerus Castle

Parish: Kilmalkedar: Cill Maeilcheadar—church of St Maolcheadair
Townland: Gallerus
O.S. map 70 ref 388 053

Near Smerwick harbour are the ruins of Gallerus Castle, which is said to have been built by the Fitzgeralds, the Knights of Kerry, late in the fifteenth or early in the sixteenth century and became one of their strongholds. Some sources say that it was built by the Fitzgeralds at a much earlier date. It was a substantial castle measuring at its base some 34 by 28 feet, and was about 50 feet in height. The stairway was at the south-east corner. The castle was five storeys high and the walls were over 7 feet thick. The upper storey rested on a stone arch.

The last Fitzgerald to live in the castle was Patrick Fitzgerald, son of the Knight. With little or no income from his smallholding, he indulged in smuggling on a grand scale with foreign ships visiting Smerwick harbour on a regular basis, bringing in goods from France and Spain. Many of the Wild Geese fled from here to France to join the Irish Brigade and never to return. Some of these were relatives of the O'Mahonys and Conways and of those whose lands had been confiscated.

The castle was later occupied by the Blennerhassetts. There is said to have been a leper colony in the vicinity in olden times. This may have been the reason the Gallerus church was built by the early monks, along with whatever other buildings existed nearby. It should be noted that leprosy was prevalent in Ireland in early times. There were many leper colonies in south Munster, too numerous to mention.

The Castles of the Kingdom

Gallarus Castle

Many tales have been related concerning the castle. Near Gallerus Castle in earlier days was a lake where a flock of wild Arctic swans came to winter each year. The arrival of these birds was supposed to be mysteriously connected to the prosperity and life of the Fitgeralds of Gallerus. When a certain number failed to arrive in late October, it was a sign or portent that a death or a serious misfortune was about to happen to the family.

The death of the last Fitzgerald who lived in the old tower house of Gallerus ended a long cycle of local history. He was the father or brother of the wives of James and Thomas Conway and Peter Ferriter. He was a proud and obstinate old man who assisted the Ferriters with their smuggling in Dingle and in Ventry and Smerwick harbours. They brought in large quantities of Bordeaux wine and Nante brandy, despite the attention of the Crown's excise men under Major Chute, who happened to be based in Dingle with over twelve men. Fitzgerald was also very active in recruiting men for the Irish Brigade in France. He lived to a great age and was confined to his bed for the final months. During his last few weeks he lay in his bed semi-conscious and was expected to pass away quietly. One night, a severe storm blew up and raged throughout the night and, as the dawn broke, to the astonishment of all his family gathered around the bed, he reared up out of bed and went to the window and threw back the timber shutters. For hours, sitting on a chair, he watched the sea in turmoil and, as the storm-force wind nearly threw him off his seat, he uttered his last words—"Tis a good day for a Geraldine to die'—and collapsed dead in his chair.

Not far from Gallerus Castle is a place on the beach known as Murrogane or Murdhucha, which can be translated as sea nymph or the place of the mermaid. We do not know if the place got its name before or after the famous tale concerning Richard Fitzgerald. It is said that, on one fine morning as he wandered along the beach, he suddenly spotted movement on a rock near the sea. As he got closer he saw a mermaid combing her long green hair, while humming some unearthly tune to herself. Nearby lay her enchanted cap. Knowing from ancient stories that if he could lay his hands on the cap she would be unable to return to the sea, he crept up and grabbed the cap before she could escape. Unable to return to the sea, she shed her tail and became a real woman. She agreed to return home with him and after a short time they got married. After about three years they had three children and were a happy family.

One day, when Richard had gone to Dingle, she found her cap hidden in the nets hanging on the wall. Beset with joy, she knew that she could return to the sea and join her family. Kissing her children goodbye and telling them that she would return, she went to the beach and, changing back to her original form, swam out to sea. When Richard returned he was informed by some people that his wife had been seen running to the shore. Realising that the magic cap had gone from its hiding place, he knew that she had returned to the sea. During the following years he waited and waited but she never returned.

There are many more tales involving mermaids around the Kerry coast. Some relate that they have been seen on the beaches shedding their skins in late September, and how the people watched for them to return to claim them again. Also, there are many stories of fishermen who had seen seals with human faces surfacing near their boats while fishing.

Glanalappa Castle
Caislean Gleann na Leapan Thoir
Parish: Knockanure: Cnoc an Ihbhair—hill of the yew tree
Townland: Glennalappa East
Location: about 4 kilometres north-east of Newtownsands village
O.S. map 64 ref 105 410

This castle was set on a huge mound beside the Owenmoy stream, which protected it in a semicircle. The Tourist Authority report of 1943 describes traces of a substantial dyke around the remaining part, indicating a large and impressive structure.

According to John O'Donovan (1841), the site revealed small sections of the walls, which were 7 feet thick. From the amount of rubble, he judged that it was a substantial tower house which was surrounded by a trench. This is now filled up and no visible sign of the castle remains. In 1943, there was no local history or folklore available, with 'even the oldest resident having nothing definite to relate'.

The castle was probably built by the O'Connor Kerrys, according to Curry and O'Donovan. The district of Myvane/Knockanure was part of the family heritage of the O'Connors of Carrignafoyle castle. They built at least one more castle in the area, including Ahalana Castle.

The location of the castle is in a glen, which has the usual fantastic stories of great fairs and impossible horse jumps from various points where riding competitions were held in past times. The townland name may refer to the hoof marks of horses or paw marks of racing wolfhounds in ancient times.

Glandine Castle
Glandeline Castle
An Gleann Doimhin
Parish: Kilgobban
Townland: Glandine
O.S. map 71 ref 705 085

Cusack in 1871 mentions a Glandine castle that existed in Glandine townland 'further up the glen' from the ruins of Camp Castle. It was situated in a commanding position overlooking Glenfais.

In 1610, Edmund Fitzjohn Fitzgerald seized the castle and the townlands. His grandsons, Morris and Edmund, forfeited all in 1653 to John Carrick, Captain Welstead and Anthony Shortcliffe. In 1731, the castle was almost totally destroyed.

Kilcushnan Castle
Parish: Ballycushlane: Baile an Chaisleain—town of the castle
Townland: Kilcusnan
Location: 3.5 kilometres north-west of Castleisland

The location of the castle is very close to Ballymacadam, Ballyplimmoth and Kilmurray castles. According to O'Donovan, when he was writing about this castle, it was an extensive ruin, which in his estimation consisted of a court and two castles—one at the east end of the court and the other attached to the south wall. The length from east to west on the inside was some 48 feet and the breadth about 21 feet. The walls were very strong and about 8 feet thick. The existing height at that time was some 45 feet. There were two fireplaces and a chimney in the west wall, while on the east wall there are three fireplaces. There were three floors in the court and castle at the east end. The other tower measured about 16 feet by over 12 feet.

This was possibly a fourth Geraldine castle in this particular area and it was probably the main castle for a period of time.

Killaha Castle
Glen Castle of the O'Donoghues
Parish: Killaha: Cill Atha—church of the ford
Townland: Killaha: Ceall Achaidh—church of St Abann
Location: 10 kilometres south-east of Killarney
O.S. map 79 ref 048 864

This was a late tower house built in the latter part of the fifteenth century and it became the seat of the O'Donoghue of the Glens. Built on the south side of the Crohan-Glen-Flesk mountain on rising ground, it guarded the entrance to this important pass not far from the Pap Mountains, which were known in ancient times as 'Da Chich Danainne' (the two paps of Danann). It became known as Killaha Castle of the O'Donoghues.

It was a substantial building, measuring at its base some 52 feet by 37 feet, with walls 8 feet thick and an overall height of some 60 feet. This was set within a large bawn, 185 feet by 120 feet. The doorway was on the east side and the spiral stairway was in the north-east corner. It was a substantial tower house of five storeys with four mantle pieces carved from ornamental limestone. The north wall no longer stands. To the left, entering the doorway, is a cell or dungeon measuring about 12 feet by 10 feet. There are no stone arches, so it is assumed that it had wooden floors.

In about 1640, a fortified house was added to the original tower. Around this time the incumbent O'Donoghue was considered a tyrannical monster. He maintained a chamber in the cellar known as the 'Black Hole', where anyone who crossed him was tortured and killed.

The castle was attacked by Ludlow in 1641 and a lot of damage was caused by cannon fire. Before this event Killaha was famous for its great parties and feasts during the time of Geoffrey O'Donoghue.

Windele (1849) says that the south-east angle tower had recently collapsed and that, in clearing the rubble, the then owner discovered a 'guard chamber' beside the entrance and beneath the floor were found some remains of a massive coffin and some human bones.

The lands of Killaha and Glen Flesk were confiscated from the O'Donoghues by Cromwell and assigned to various Englishmen. It seems probable that these people never took up the option of ownership and the O'Donoghues retained possession for a time.

Killorglin Castle
Castle Conway—Caislean Cille Forgla
Parish: Killorglin: Cill Fhorgal—church of St Forgla
Townland: Killorglin
Location: in the centre of Killorglin, on a hill overlooking the bridge over the Laune River
O.S. map 78 ref 776 965

Nothing remains of the old castle, which was built early in the thirteenth century by Maurice Fitz-thomas Fitzgerald. It became one of the manors of the Earl of Desmond and was known as the manor house of the Desmonds before Tralee Castle. After the Anglo-Normans gained control of large areas of North Kerry in 1214, the rents of the Iveragh peninsula were paid to the chief of the Geraldines at Killorglin Castle. It changed hands many times during the turbulent years that followed.

The castle was attacked and burned by the MacCarthys after the Battle of Callan in 1261. It was handed by the Fitzgeralds, together with its manor, to the Knights Templar at some time and they retrieved it when the Templar Order was dissolved early in the fourteenth century.

In the hands of the MacCarthys, it was repaired and occupied again. During the Desmond wars it suffered another attack and was almost totally destroyed. Under confiscation, the castle and lands were held by a Captain Jenkyn Conway and a number of soldiers. His son, under the conditions of possession, was obliged to build another castle under James I *c.* 1613.

Using the stones of the old castle, a mansion house was built after the Williamite wars by Robert Blennerhassett, who had married Avis Conway. He became a member of parliament for the borough of Tralee in 1634.

The Blennerhassetts, who later owned the town, changed the name to Castle Conway *c.* 1796, then sold the place to Thomas Mullins of Burnham, who was later to become the first Lord Ventry. Nothing now remains of this later castle except a gable-end, even though it was occupied up to the 1830s. The remains stand on the north side of Lower Bridge Street in Killorglin.

Liscahane Castle
Liscahaune Castle/Fort of the O'Kanes

Parish: Ardfert: Árd Fhearta—height of the grave
Townland: Lis Cahane—fort of the O'Kanes
Location: in the Barony of Clanmaurice, 2 kilometres south of Ardfert
O.S. map 71 ref 790 190

Nothing now remains of this castle. It is as if it had never existed. However, there is a reference in the *Four Masters* stating that, in 1600, a strong castle, which was held by John Óg Morris Fitzmaurice, existed in Ardfert. This family was probably related to the Castle of Lixnaw. The sources say that later it was garrisoned by the Earl of Thomond.

In 1598, the castle was in the hands of Edward Gray on behalf of Sir Edward Denny of Tralee and Sir Charles Walsingham and their associates. It was taken by the Irish in the rebellion of that year from this Edward Gray, but two years later, in 1600, it was reoccupied by Maurice Stack, who was serving under Sir George Carew, whose army swept through Kerry. He occupied the castle for a number of years. It was later occupied by a Richard Gunn during the rebellion of 1641 and subsequently by a Richard Birch took over the occupancy.

It was described by Carew as a poor little castle and was probably of no great importance, as it had no strategic location.

Listowel Castle
Lios Tuathail—Fort of the O'Toole

Parish: Listowel: Lios Tuathail—fort of Tuathal
Townland: Listowel
Location: centre of Listowel
O.S. map 63 ref 989 335

This castle was probably built by the Fitzmaurices or by another prominent local family called the MacElligotts. The castle was the stronghold of the Lords of Kerry—Clanmaurice. Situated on the north side of the river Feale on a high bank overlooking the river and the town of Listowel, it is still an imposing structure and is in fairly good condition. The approximate date of building is roughly the end of the fifteenth century. There is a possibility that there was an earlier castle built on roughly the same site. What we see today appears as a twin tower fifteenth-century castle with a broad arch like Bunratty Castle.

Originally it was probably a square castle with a tower at each corner. What we see now is only one side, consisting of two square towers of about 50 feet connected by a wall of the same height and spanned by an arch on top. The castle itself extended between the two towers towards the bank of the river. What remained of this part was taken down in the nineteenth century. The towers and wall are built of limestone with lime and sand mortar and ascend to a height of about 50 feet. The work is grouted. Between the arch and the wall there is a space through which stones, boiling water and other missiles were thrown down on those who attacked the castle. The tower on the west side has no means of ascending to the chambers above, so access must have been through another tower which no longer exists.

In the wall there used to be a projecting stone with the remains of a face carved into it which was said to be that of

LISTOWEL CASTLE

the 'Architect' MacElligott. Alternatively, the sculpture may be of an ape to commemorate Thomas an Apa, son of Maurice Fitzthomas and father of the first Earl of Desmond, who, according to legend, was cared for as an infant, after the battle of Callan, by an ape that was a pet of the family. Of course, it is possible that this whole story is a later invention and there is some doubt as to whether the name 'an Apa' was applied to Thomas during his lifetime.

Listowel Castle was at least partially demolished by the Fitzmaurices in 1582 to prevent its use by the enemy. However, it was still in Irish hands up to 1600 when its garrison of only eighteen men surrendered to Sir George Carew's army, which was under the command of Sir Charles Wilmot. This was the last castle to hold out against the forces of Elizabeth I. The small garrison finally surrendered when they saw that the walls had been seriously undermined by the besiegers. The men of the garrison pleaded for their lives but Wilmot would only state that, if they surrendered before they were blown up, their fate would be at his discretion. After they surrendered and begged for their lives on bended knees, nine were hanged immediately, this being equivalent to the losses on the besieging side. The women and children within were allowed to go free, but the rest of the armed garrison were later executed. The eldest son of the Lord of Kerry escaped, but the lad of five was later captured by treachery and handed over to the Lord President, who dispatched him to England.

Lord Listowel bought the manorial rights from Lord Kerry. These were later purchased by Richard Hare in 1783.

For a long time, Listowel was a castle surrounded by a cluster of buildings rather than a town as such. The town developed after the fall of the castle.

The river is called Abainn feile—Feale river. It is said that Fial, wife of Lughadh, died of fright here by the riverside in ancient times.

Letter Castle
Litter Castle—MacCrehin's Castle
Parish: Caher: Chathair—stone fort
Townland: Letter
O.S. map 83 ref 474 770

Litter or Letter Castle was, according to Smith, in the same parish as Ballycarbery Castle, otherwise known as Caher Castle, and belonged to the MacCrohan branch of the O'Sullivan Mórs, whose territory stretched from Cahirciveen to Reencarragh point. This branch was always loyal to the clan leader so must have taken his side in all warfare and rebellions.

The castle must have been built on the site of an ancient well-known fort but has completely vanished off the face of the earth. However, the site is known to those living in the vicinity.

Litter Castle
Letter—Littir Castle—An Leitir
Parish: Aghavallen: Acha Mhala or maybe Paraise na h-Uachomhala
Townland: Letter: Leitir—hillside
Location: approximately 2.75 kilometres north-west of Astee, near Letter Point (the exact location of this castle is unknown)
O.S. map 63 ref 925 477

Litter castle is shown on a 1750s map of Kerry, where it is placed to the east of Beal Castle.

It is understood that it was a stronghold of the O'Connors and then of the Fitzmaurice family. It is said to have been located along the south bank at the entrance of the Shannon river near the sea.

Lixnaw Castle

Parish: Kilcara: Cill Charthaigh—church of St Carthach
Townland: Lixnaw: Leac Snamha—flagstone of the swimming
Location: 1 kilometre west of Lixnaw village on the road to Ballinclogher
O.S. map 71 ref 892 292

The original castle is reputed to have been built in the twelfth or early in the thirteenth century by Maurice, second Lord of Kerry. This family also built the old bridge here as early as 1320. He held a strong position in the model parliament under Edward I in England and married a Scottish woman from a strong Scottish clan, who were trying to make peace with the English Crown before William Wallace came on the scene. The castle was built on high ground close to the river Brick. It is believed to have been a strong square castle. The general outline of the castle is visible today. A surrounding mound, which measures approximately 95 feet by 115 feet, encloses the site.

At the south-east corner is what is referred to as the Cock House, which dates from the seventeenth century. The whole area is enclosed by at least four raised mounds. Nothing is left of the castle, yet there are remains of the mansion house of the earls of Kerry, which was built nearby. The castle saw plenty of action over the centuries. In 1568, while in the possession of Thomas Fitzmaurice, Lord of Kerry, it was attacked by James Fitzmaurice Fitzgerald, his cousin. After a brief encounter, James, son and heir of Garrett Fitzgerald, lay dead.

In 1600, when the Fitzmaurices revolted against the Crown, Sir Charles Wilmot attacked the castle. The defenders had undermined the castle ready for demolition but Wilmot's forces took them by surprise, captured the castle and made it their base for operating in the surrounding countryside. Lord Kerry recaptured the castle and held off Wilmot's troops. He then entrusted the castle to his brother Gerald, who was forced to surrender through lack of drinking water. Fitzmaurice made peace with the Crown in 1601 and was regranted his north Kerry estates, but, when the Spaniards arrived at Kinsale in 1601, the clan took up arms again and once more revolted. In 1603, King James pardoned Fitzmaurice and his lands were again regranted.

Not far away stands a tower on a rounded hill, where the second last of the earls of Kerry lies interred.

Old Court/Lixnaw House

In the context of Lixnaw Castle we have to mention the Old Court, which was a very large structure built in the seventeenth or the eighteenth century that replaced Lixnaw Castle. This was the abode of the Fitzmaurices. Thomas Fitzmaurice became the twenty-first Lord Kerry and, in 1697, he married Anne Petty, the daughter of Sir William Petty, who was continually increasing his fortune. Anne was instrumental in the building of an extensive mansion, sparing no expense. It is said to have rivalled Buckingham Palace in its heyday.

It was a large long oblong building running north to south and had 6-foot windows on each side wall. The east wall was buttressed and had a number of fireplaces. According to Smith *c.* 1756, the house contained a large building with wings at either side and some other buildings. In one of the wings was a chapel with full-sized frescoes. The interior was lavishly decorated.

The hermitage or castle

This was probably a defensive outpost for Old Court and was built around the same time. The tower is approximately 52 feet by 30 feet outside. There are four arched cellars beneath the first floor but these are not connected to each other. However, there was a passageway running north to south for a distance of about 42 feet, which was about 4 feet wide. All the cellars had slit windows, probably for defence purposes.

Minegahane Castle
Parish: Killoory: Cill Luraigh—church of St Lurach
Townland: Meenogahane: Min O'gCathain—strip of level land of the O'Cathains
Location: slightly to the east of Castle Shannon and 5 kilometres west of Rattoo
O.S. map 63 ref 798 345

The fable of Scylla seems to be associated with this castle. Built on a rocky outcrop overlooking the sea, it is noted for its nearby caves, which emit a sound like the firing of cannons when there is bad weather and a heavy swell.

There was a rare reference to this castle in the *Civil Survey* of 1664–6, where it is described as being built inside a promontory ring-fort or rath. It was already long in ruins by 1658, when there was a description of a ruined house, some cabins and the butt of an old castle.

In recent years the site was examined by John Pierce of Listowel, who found that the remains suggested there had been a rectangular building of about 32 feet by 7 feet, with indications of a square tower measuring about 8 feet by 14 feet at the south end. This section was about 14 feet high and contained some ten steps. This would point to it having been a small tower house.

The Pierces, who were related to the Fitzmaurices, lived

in this area from around the fourteenth century. After the Cromwellian confiscations, they were transported to Connaught where they remained for some time before returning c. 1700. In Kerry history, the castle was well known as a smuggler base where wines, brandy and goods from France and Spain were landed into its labyrinth of caves, which had steps and landing places for small boats. These have now been worn away by the action of the sea.

Minard Castle
Caislean na Minairde/Caislean an Muraig in Cille Cuain
Parish: Minard: Min Árd: Cill Mhuire
Townland: Minard
O.S. map 70 ref 555 992

Here is another castle that was built on an ancient promontory fort. It was a large tower house and the largest castle built by the Geraldines, indeed it was more like a fortress. It was probably the last Fitzgerald castle built on the Dingle peninsula in the second half of the sixteenth century. Built of roughly shaped sandstone blocks and split stone, and with a core of rubble, chippings and beach pebbles laid in strong mortar, it was built to withstand any attack.

The ruins of the castle stand on the edge of the sea. All the walls except the east still stand and are about 50 feet high. It was a large castle measuring 50 feet by 41 feet. It had two stone arches and there were five storeys—one under the bottom arch, three between arches and one over the top arch. The stairway was at the south-east corner.

In 1650, Walter Hussey defended the castle against the

Michael J Carroll

MINARD CASTLE KILMURRY

parliamentary forces of Le Hunt and Sadler. These two had the castle bombarded by English warships, while they built a fortification from which they could fire cannon shots. The remains of this fortification still existed in 1837. The cannon fire did not make much of an impression on the castle, so powder kegs were placed in the lower vault in order to blow up the castle, with a serious loss of life amongst the defenders, who had been reduced to making pewter shot from melted down knives and forks. Hussey's body was identified by the red stocking he wore around his neck, like a scarf, as a mark of distinction.

Not very far from the site of the castle, an earlier battle was fought between the Knight of Kerry and Sir Charles Wilmot.

Coom na Muice Dubh is located not far from the castle.

Molahiffe Castle
Magh Laithimh Castle—Molahiff Castle
Parish: Molahiffe: Magh Laithimh—plain of Laithemh (Lahiff)
Townland: Castlefarm
Location: 1.5 kilometres north of Fieries village
O.S. map 71 ref 912 046

The ruins of this castle stand in the grounds of Castlefarm House. The material for its construction is said to have come from a nearby ancient stone fort.

The castle was built on a high rock in the middle of the plain. Only part of the south-east corner remains, to a height of about 55 feet. The walls were 8 feet thick. According to tradition, this castle was built by the MacCarthys. It is mentioned as the seat of Teige, the son of Dermot MacCarthy, in early historical reports. Teige was killed at Aghadoe in the Earl of Desmond's camp by Captain Siuiti during a vicious argument. It is stated in the *Annals of Innisfallen* that the castle was originally built by the son of Maurice Fitzgerald. However, this does not correspond in history, as *that* Maurice Fitzgerald died in 1306, which would put the building of the castle at *c.* 1280 onwards.

An alternative theory is that the castle was built by the Geraldines *c.* 1217. Thomas Fitzmaurice had acquired the surrounding land from King John *c.* 1215. After the Geraldine defeat at Callan, this plus the other castles on the Maine river were held by the Sliocht Owen Mór MacCarthy of Cois Mainge. This particular sept held the land or the border (i.e., the river Maine dividing the territories of the MacCarthys and the Fitzgeralds). Having divided into three minor septs, each held one of the castles.

A John and William Brown forfeited the castle in 1563. It was then held by Owen Mór MacCarthy until 1583, when it was forfeited after the Geraldine rebellion and placed in the hands of Sir Valentine Brown as steward of all the lands of Owen MacCormac and John Ulick. These lands and castles, in addition to the territory of O'Donoghue Mór, later became part of the Kenmare estate of the Browns. The castle was the residence of Lord Kenmare from 1587 until Killarney House was built. The Browns married into the O'Sullivans, MacCarthys and the Fitzgeralds and became Catholics.

Nearby Fieries and Clonmellane castles, which are also situated near the banks of the river Maine, were MacCarthy castles and, by 1837, belonged to the Browns of Kenmare.

Moorstown Castle
Castle Moore
Parish: Kilquan: Cill Chuain—church of St Cuan
Townland: Moorstown
Location: close to Feohanagh village
O.S. map 70 ref 403 099

This castle was built on a low rock and was about 60 feet high. The walls were over 6 feet thick and built of red sandstone. The lack of remains gives little information about its original size, but it seems to have been quite a substantial tower house. One local name is 'Caislean na gCuig gCuinne' (i.e., the five-cornered castle).

A substantial portion was extant in 1841 but the plan could not be determined. The perilous condition of the remains resulted in their being knocked down in 1921. Only a small section of one wall remains.

This was probably a fine five-storey tower house. There is no date of construction but it is reputed to have been built by the Fitzgeralds in the fifteenth century. It is related that the son of this Fitzgerald fell to his death from the roof and the family abandoned the castle believing it to be cursed.

A short time later, the Moores moved into the castle as tenants and almost immediately bitterness began between themselves and the Hoares of Castle Gregory concerning the boundary between their property.

The castle is marked on a map of 1550 and also on 'The Rough Draght of Mounster' of 1576.

Palice Castle
Caislean Ua Cartha
Caislean na Pailisi/Pallis mhic Carthaigh
Known as Pallas Castle
Parish: Aghadoe: Achadh-Dá Eó—field of the two yews
Townland: Pallis: Pailise—palace
Location: west of Fossa on the road from Killarney to Killorglin
O.S. map 78 ref 884 932

In 1840, the ruined Palice Castle stood on high ground in the centre of the townland with a full view of the Gap of Dunloe and Laune bridge. About 5 feet of the north wall angle could still be seen. The walls were about 6 feet thick and the building measured about 35 feet by 20, which is small for a tower house.

This castle was the residence of the chieftain MacCarthy Mór and his descendants and, like all seats of the main clans, it had an area in front where the chief held court. This particular area was called 'Pairce-an-Crochadh' (the gallows field). This small castle was held by the MacCarthy Mórs for about three hundred years. In 1588, it was described as the chief house of MacCarthy Mór. It could not be described as a palace, as the accommodation was more than sparse and had two thatched outbuildings alongside.

In 1510, the Lord Chief Justice of Ireland, Garrett, Earl of Kildare, with the English and Irish nobles of Leinster marched with a large army into Munster. Besides taking many castle they also gained Palice Castle.

According to Smith, the MacCarthys built a more modern residence nearby and called it New Palace, and this was still standing in 1750.

The folklore of the district relates stories of the castle's vaulted passageways, which were either used as escape tunnels or as a place of refuge when the castle was attacked.

The Cromwellian forces largely destroyed the castle and later, in 1837, the remains were knocked down at night by a contractor and the stones used to repair a nearby road.

As a result of a decree of the Court of Claims in London dated 28 July 1663, the lands of Palice, Muckross, Harnane, Castle Lough and other lands were restored to Dame Sarah MacCarthy, daughter of the Earl of Antrim and widow of Daniel MacCarthy Mór. The second son of Dame Sarah, Florence, sold Cahirnane Castle and lands to Maurice Hussey in 1684 and gave Castle Lough to his cousin Denis MacCarthy.

The O'Dalys were poets to MacCarthy Mór at Palice. They were also hereditary landholders in their own right and were entitled to the wedding dress of every girl married in Desmond. The custom was to claim the dress on the wedding day so that there was no chance of it getting damaged or spoiled. Many a young bride was left in her petticoats or less before the wedding feast had even started.

Pookeenee Castle
Poulaninneen Castle
Parish: Killehenny/Killahinny: Cill Eithne—church of St Eithne
Townland: Scoltnadrida
O.S. map 63 ref 862 424

This castle was situated very close to Ballybunion and Doon castles, a little bit north of Ballybunion town, on the southern side of Doon Cove, within the confines of a large promontory fort. It seems to have derived its name from a cluster of little huts (na puicini) or botháns in the immediate vicinity, or it could indicate a man who wore a patch over one eye.

This castle was but a small tower with a wall and a turret.

Access was across a neck of land. It is reputed to have been built late in the fifteenth century. According to Westropp (1909), the tower at the end of the south wall had three small vaulted chambers in the lower floor. Poulaninneen (the pool of the nine daughters) also had three arched caves under the castle, where the sea entered at high tide. The legend of the caves is that the daughters of the local chieftain tried to elope with some Danish prisoners but they were all drowned during the attempt.

There were traces of a wooden and earthen hall attached to the tower, which measured about 17 feet at the south wall and was over 4 feet thick.

Punt Castle
Portrinarde Castle
Parish: Duagh (Dooagh): Dubh-Ath—the black ford

This castle was situated near Abbeyfeale and it was reputed to have been built by Nicholas, the third Lord Kerry, who died in 1324 and was later interred in Ardfert friary (see King). Almost nothing is known about this castle but it must have been situated near the site of the much later Duagh House.

The fifth Lord Kerry, John, married an Elinor Pierce of Ballymacaquim Castle. As a result of the Desmond rebellion these Fitzmaurices lost their castle and territory. However, they recovered most of them later only to lose them again in the Cromwellian confiscations. Following the Restoration, Ulick Fitzmaurice received a regrant of his lands. For his part in the Williamite war another Fitzmaurice lost the lands again but they were restored to the family, as they had been left to a grandson by Ulick Fitzmaurice's wife.

Rahinane Castle
Rathinaun Castle or Rahinnane Castle
Parish: Ventry: Fionn Traigh—white strand
Townland: Rahinaun: Ráth Fhionain—fort of Fionann
Location: road from Ventry to Ballyferriter about 3 kilometres from Ventry village
O.S. map 70 ref 369 017

This castle was built in a large ancient rath surrounded by ditches and mounds on high ground overlooking Carrahane Bay or Ventry harbour. It measured approximately 40 by 28 feet at its base and was about 60 feet high. The first floor was built over an arch. The doorway was on the south-west side and a stone stairway ran upwards through the 6-foot wall. There are no indications of a fireplace. On the doorway to the stairs there is an arch and on the west wall the remains of a garderobe. The windows were very plain.

A substantial amount of the castle ruins still stand. It appears to have been a square tower house built inside the site of an ancient ring fort, so that it was surrounded by a very large defensive bank of earth and a deep fosse. It also had a maze of souterrains, which were probably used as a refuge or a means of escape.

The eastern wall suffered severe damage, probably from an attack, although the possibility of cannon fire from a ship in Ventry harbour is unlikely, due to the distance. The castle was built some time in the fifteenth century by the knights of Kerry and this family lived there for many centuries. John Fitzgerald of Rahinane, the second knight, joined the Desmond rebellion. He somehow managed to get a pardon. Again he rebelled and joined the Irish forces at the battle of Kinsale in 1601. In 1603, he again went into rebellion, but was pardoned by James I. He tried to remain neutral during

Michael J Carroll

RAHINNANE CASTLE

the Cromwellian wars. Maurice Fitzgerald married Elizabeth Crosbie in 1703 and became a Protestant. Shortly after that the castle was abandoned and fell into ruin.

In old times no one would visit the castle vicinity at midnight for fear of seeing a ghost which was often reported to be wandering around the castle ruins. No history or folklore exists about any murder or atrocity in the castle to account for this malevolent ghost.

Rahoneen Castle

Parish: Ardfert: Árd Fheart—height of the grave
Townland: Rahoneen: Ráth Eoin Óg—fort of young Eoin
Location: west of Ardfert near Carrahane strand
O.S. map 71 ref 759 202

This square castle, standing on the edge of a cliff, was about 30 feet by 20 feet at its base and was probably built c. 1311 by the O'Leyne or O'Laoghain and destroyed in 1637. Much of the remains tumbled down the side of the hill where it was located. A small section of the wall remained standing, about 28 feet high. It is reputed to have been destroyed by the Cromwellian forces. There are various references suggesting it may once have been a residence of the Bishops of Ardfert.

In 1661, a juror of the Inquisition was Christopher Willoe of Rahoneen Castle, so part of the castle may still have been habitable at that time.

Michael J Carroll

RAHONEEN (BISHOPS) CASTLE

Ratass Castle
Hollenhone Castle
Also known as Ballingowan Castle
Parish: Ratass: Ráth Teas—southern fort
Townland: Ballingowan/Ballygobbin: Baile an Gobhan—townland of the smith
Location: 2.5 kilometres east of Tralee

This was reputed to have been a strong castle of the Desmonds, which commanded the route from Tralee to Castleisland. Now, however, nothing remains.

The earliest date given relating to this castle was that it was burned by the O'Briens in 1138, but this could be a misprint and should perhaps read 1238. Otherwise it would be one of the earliest castles built in Kerry, well before the Anglo-Normans' arrival in the county.

The next mention of the castle is that Dermot MacTurlough O'Connor occupied the castle in 1608, but the castle and lands were forfeited by his son Tirlogh O'Connor late in 1641. In 1688, Terence Óg O'Connor was in possession of Ratass Castle.

Walter, grandson of Walter Hussey of Minard Castle, lived in the castle early in the eighteenth century, but possibly in a newly built house rather than the castle proper. Smith refers to Ballingowan as the seat of the Rice-Morris family in 1756. It is said that it was later occupied by a Francis Pepys *c.* 1768.

Rathmorrel Castle
D'Cantillon's Castle
Parish: Killoory: Cill Luraigh—church of St Lurach
Townland: Rathmorrel: Ráth Muralaigh
Location: near Ballyheigue
O.S. map 71 ref 792 296

It is said that this was a Norman castle built by the D'Cantillon family some time in the thirteenth century.

O'Donovan states that it was a rectangular building with some of the walls still remaining to about 20 feet in height in 1841.

A few remains can still be seen close to the present Rathmorrel House.

Rattoo Castle
Parish: Rattoo: Ráth Thuaidh—the north fort
Townland: Rattoo
Location: 8 kilometres east of Minegahane Castle
O.S. map 63 ref 880 335

The precise location of this castle is unknown today, as it has been completely demolished. Originally it was a stronghold of the Fitzgeralds, earls of Desmond and lords of Kerry. Sir Charles Wilmot captured the castle and placed a garrison there in 1600. The nearby abbey was set on fire by the fleeing Irish troops. Wilmot also captured Abbeyfeale at this time.

In 1608, Dermot MacTurlough O'Connor was in possession of the castle and lands. Later in 1641 all was forfeited by his son Tirlogh. Later, in the early eighteenth century, another Walter Hussey, who was a grandson of Walter Hussey of Minard Castle, lived at Rattoo.

Reenavanig Castle
Reenavanny
Rinn na mBan Oige—headland of the young women
Townland: Reenavanig: Whiddy Island: Oilean Faoide
Parish: Kilmacomogue, Bantry—church of Young St Colman
O.S. map 85 ref 975 508

This small tower house was erected at the north-east end of the island by Dermod O'Sullivan *c.* 1473. This key position on Whiddy Island at the entrance to the inner harbour meant that a castle located here would have protected the shipping and fishing rights of the clan and enabled them to levy duties on trading vessels. When the O'Sullivan territory was divided in 1593, the island was declared part of Sir Owen's lands, and a short time later he mortgaged it to Hugh Broigley and James Derbyshire.

When Mountjoy's forces of approximately 2,000 men arrived in Bantry in 1602 on their way to Dunboy, over half of them were billeted on the island near the castle. Donal Cam O'Sullivan was informed of their position and immediately gathered two hundred and fifty of his best men. Under cover of darkness, they made their way by sea and landed on the north side of the island in darkness and surprised the English just as dawn was breaking. Fearing that they were being attacked by a superior Irish force, Mountjoy's men abandoned their camp and headed for the shore, leaving their baggage and muskets behind. Had it not been for the timely arrival of several boats and barges, the greater part of them would have been killed or drowned. As it was, about two hundred of them are estimated to have perished in the short skirmish.

After this disaster, Carew ordered that Reenavanig Castle be destroyed on his return from the victory of Dunboy. The one wall that remained standing collapsed during the gales of 1920 and only about 20 feet survive, with signs of a lintelled window and rows of joist holes. It is said that the ground floor of the castle was used as a prison. Near the ruins are the control tower and the American seaplane base which were operational at the end of the First World War. Nothing remains of the ancient priory of St Canera that gave the castle its name.

Ross Castle
Parish: Killarney: Cill Airne—church of St Airne/Athairhe
Townland: Ross Island
O.S. map 78 ref 949 887

This famous castle was built in the fourteenth or early in the fifteenth century and is a strong keep with later additions. The castle is a tall battlemented building on limestone rock. At the north-west side it is support by a massive buttress and has two machicolated defences projecting from the south-east and north-west angles near the top. It was formerly enclosed by a curtain wall, with rounded flankers at each corner.

The interior of the castle is arched at about two-thirds of its height. It consisted of four floors—ground floor, two wooden floors, which were supported by beams of timber, and the top floor resting on a stone arch. The north wall had narrow windows, while the east had a large square window. The upper apartment, known as O'Donoghue's dining-room,

The Castles of the Kingdom

measures some 34 feet by 20 feet and contained (1849) a large fireplace with a marble mantel. A spiral stairway runs to the top of the castle and the walls are just over 4 feet thick.

In the early nineteenth century there was a barracks attached to the west side. Lord Kenmare, in the 1840s, bowed to popular demand and had this made into a picturesque ruin.

Ross Castle was founded by the O'Donoghue family and for nearly three hundred years was the residence of the prince of the lakes, who became known as the O'Donoghue of Ross. O'Donoghue was noted throughout Ireland for having the best wine cellar in the country, after the Franciscan monastery in Bantry where, in 1601, Donal Cam ordered his men to axe every barrel in case they fell into the hands of the English forces. It is said that, when the men had finished their work, the wine and brandy came up to their knees and when they came up out of the cellar they were completely intoxicated by the fumes.

The O'Donoghue possessions were confiscated as a result of their part in the Desmond rebellion but MacCarthy Mór, who had sided with the English, contested the arrangement and retrieved the property. He later decided to mortgage it to Sir Valentine Brown, who in 1620 received the regrant of about 90,000 acres around Killarney, which were previously in the hands of the families of MacCarthy Mór, O'Donoghue Mór and the Earl of Desmond. In 1689, he became the Baron of Castleross and Viscount Kenmare.

Ross Castle stands on so-called Ross Island, which in fact is connected to the mainland and is just a promontory, a narrow neck of land jutting out into Loch Lein. The access was trenched across to afford extra protection to the castle in earlier days. Further out is the small rock named O'Donoghue's Prison Rock, where the chieftain imprisoned and kept confined his rebellious son and his associates. His son was called Teighe Mergach (angry one), as he was prone to break out in to severe bouts of anger.

St Leger in 1589 described Ross as the strongest sanctuary of a castle built in Ireland and as almost impregnable. The castle played a big part in the Cromwellian war. After the defeat of the Royalist forces in County Cork in 1652, Lord Muskerry withdrew to the castle with what remained of his forces, thinking that he could resist Ludlow's forces or a siege for at least two years.

Part of the legend or prophecy concerning Ross Castle is as follows:

> 'Till Barnam Wood meets Dunsinane
> Macbeth before no foe shall quail,
> And Ross may all assault disdain,
> Till on Loch Lein strange ship shall sail.

We do not know if Ludlow knew about this ancient prophecy or not. However, he gave orders that ships be built by Captain Thomas Chudleigh of Kinsale. These were taken aboard frigates that landed at Castlemaine harbour and were

The Castles of the Kingdom

ROSS CASTLE

then pulled up the river Laune by bullocks and manpower until they arrived at Loch Lein. This was a repetition of what happened in 1152 when the Moriartys, with the aid of the O'Connors of Connaught, pulled boats up the river and then overland on special carts to the lake to attack the O'Donoghue castle.

It is not known how many boats were transported in this manner and put together, or how many cannons they could carry. Yet, when they appeared on Loch Lein in the early morning mist of 22 June 1652, Ross Castle, with over two thousand soldiers within its confines, surrendered without a struggle. This was the last fortress in Munster to fall to the Cromwellian forces.

The Browns retained the lands and the castle but built a mansion nearby in 1688. The castle became a military barracks until the nineteenth century.

Loch Lein is divided into a lower, middle and upper lake. It takes its name from Lein, who was a famous metalworker noted for making gold ornaments in ancient times.

Another legend relates how the famous Prince O'Donoghue, chieftain of the lakes, consulted books of black magic and used strange potions in an attempt to regain his lost youth. On one occasion, while he was reading a magic book, all the devils of the world appeared in his chamber at the top of the castle. There was a noise as if the whole castle would fall to pieces. When his wife saw her child dead on the table, she let out a horrendous shriek, which caused the castle to sway from side to side. In panic, O'Donoghue jumped out of a window and disappeared below the surface of the lake. His horse, his table and his books all were whisked away at the same moment. The story goes that he lives on in a lively palace at the bottom of the loch and that every seventh year he can be seen riding his charger with silver hooves across the windswept lake.

Muckross Abbey

It is generally believed that the monks were expelled from Muckross during Elizabeth's reign. However, there was an instruction on 24 August 1542 that 'A commission be set up directing the Earl of Desmond, Thomas A'Garde, Eneas O'Hernan and Edmund Sextone to take inventories of all religious houses in the counties of Cork, Kerry, Limerick and Desmond, to dissolve the same, and put them in safe custody for the King' (Henry VIII).

Note: when Ross Castle was taken by the Cromwellian forces in 1652, the monks of Innisfallen were expelled from their monastery.

Short Castle: No. 1
Srugreena Castle—Caislean Gearr
Parish: Killinane: Cill Lonain—church of St Lonan
Townland: Glebe or Srugreena
O.S. map 83 ref 532 795

This castle was located a short distance south-east of Killinane Church, which is now a ruin, and what still exists is in the burial ground. Almost nothing of the building remained at the turn of the last century, only a butt of a corner wall.

Srugreena Castle (Sroughrone) was situated in ancient Desmond territory, south of the river Fearta, and was supposed to have been occupied by a branch of the MacCarthys who were descendants of the old MacCarthy Trant family. The family lost possession of the castle and lands after the rebellion of 1641 but succeeded in getting them back on lease in 1697. One of the MacCarthys, Daniel of Srugreena, died in 1752.

A late Victorian or Edwardian house—Srugreena Abbey—once occupied the site but has since completely disappeared. There are fragmentary remains of the MacCarthy Trant house which preceded the abbey. There are also a holy well and a mass rock in the vicinity.

Short Castle: No. 2
Parish: Knockane: Cnocan—small hillock
Townland: Beaufort
O.S. map 78 ref 882 922

This castle was situated between Aghadoe and the Gap of Dunloe. Its site was, by 1849, occupied by Beaufort House. The location was near Beaufort bridge by the river Laune and it was probably built to guard the crossing across the river before the bridge was constructed.

Beaufort House is a regency mansion, which was built over a partial basement. This was probably one of several tower houses along the river. After the Cromwellian wars it was in the hands of John Walsh, although the castle was probably already in ruins. The construction of a large farmhouse on the site began in the late seventeenth or early eighteenth century.

Short Castle: No. 3
Also called Rice Castle
Parish: Tralee: Traighlí—strand of Lee
Townland: Tralee

This castle has now completely disappeared. It was situated where the Bank of Ireland building now stands. Originally it was one of the castles of the Knight of

Kerry. As Tralee was never a walled town, there were many castles built in its vicinity for defensive purposes.

In January 1642, the castle was manned with guns which repelled an attack mounted on Tralee Castle (The Great Castle) by an Irish force under the command of Florence MacDaniel MacFineen Carthy during the Irish rebellion. Both Tralee castles were garrisoned by the English at this time. The close proximity of these two buildings is given credence by the story that, during this siege, the respective garrisons passed messages back and forth via a rope slung across the top of each castle on pulleys.

During the siege over 105 people took refuge in the castle. Together with the small garrison, everyone was packed into two floors which measured approximately 18 by 24 feet. One can only imagine the conditions!

The Rice family of Short Castle is said to have had another castle nearby, but I have been unable to identify its location.

See also Tralee and Castle MacEllistrim and Ardfert Castle, which was sometimes called Short Castle.

Tallagh Castle
Taulaught or Tawlaght Castle
Parish: Ballynahaglish/Churchtown/Baile na hEaglaise
Townland: Tawlaght
O.S. map 71 ref 745 165

This castle, which was situated near Chapeltown, was also called Castle MacAndrew. There are no signs of any remains.

It was situated to the south-east of the square castle of Fenit and the round castle of Barrow and still existed in 1580.

These three castles guarded Barrow harbour from pirates.

Tarbert Castle

Parish: Kilnaughtin: Cill Neachtain—church of St Neachtain
Townland: Tieraclea—land of the hurdle

Very little is known about this castle, except that it existed somewhere in Tarbert itself, probably on the north side of the square, which would have been the strongest defensible point in the area. It is known that it was built c. 1450 by the Earl of Desmond, who subsequently transferred it to James Fitzmaurice Fitzgerald. There is no mention of its existence during the Desmond wars, except that the Countess of Desmond lived there for a short period c. 1579.

Sir William Herbert held the castle, as well as most of the surrounding lands, in 1584 after the lands were confiscated. In 1589, the castle and part of the lands were assigned to a John Hollies, but he was prevented from having possession by Herbert. Patrick Crosbie resided in the castle from 1609 to 1611 and during this period he transplanted about two hundred and fifty families from Queen's County (County Laois). Sir Peter Crosbie, his son, sold the castle and the lands to Dominic Roche, who, during the Cromwellian wars, forfeited his possessions. Sir William King later became the owner. It is not known how or why the castle fell into ruins, but it must have occurred during the Cromwellian conquest.

Tarmon Castle
An Tearmann Thoir
Parish: Kilnaughtin: Cill Neachtain—church of St Neachtain
Townland: Tarmon Hill
Location: about 3 kilometres south of the port and town of Tarbert

No trace of the castle exists today but it was probably a fair-sized tower house, as Dermot, the son of John O'Connor, Lord Tarbert, is supposed to have lived there. The second and the third Lord Tarbert are reputed to have lived here until 1550.

Some sources say that it was built by the Fitzmaurices but there is a reliable reference that says that it was actually built by the O'Connor Kerrys late in the thirteenth century, when the family were trying to halt the incursion of the Anglo-Normans into their territory. It was probably the scene of many sieges and assaults during the following centuries.

Tralee

The town of Tralee was an Anglo-Norman settlement founded either by Meilor Fitzhenry or John Fitzthomas. Of interest here is the mention in one record of the defeat of Norman forces outside the settlement of Tralee by the MacCarthys and O'Driscolls from West Cork. There is no mention in other sources of the O'Driscolls participating in any Kerry battles, other than against the Vikings.

From the thirteenth century onwards, there were various castles in and around Tralee, each of which goes by a variety of names, depending on what family occupied them at any particular time. The three that stood within what is now known as Tralee town were the Great Castle of the Desmonds, the Short Castle of the Rices and Castle MacEllistrom. The last two of these are dealt with in their alphabetical place. There were two more which were located within a short distance of the town centre. In fact, there were some nineteen castles between Tralee and the county border with Cork. Amongst these could be counted Ballybeggan, Ballymullen and Ratass.

The present town is built over the sites of two castles, the Great Castle of the Desmonds and Short Castle of the Rices, and an ancient abbey and a burial ground. Some people sleep above the bodies of holy monks and brave knights of times past! The last wall of the Great Castle to fall extended about halfway across the present Denny Street, while Short Castle was where the Bank of Ireland now stands. The river Lee rose in O'Brennan's territory and ran through the parish of Ballymacelligott and, 8 miles later, ran around Desmond's Castle before entering the sea. Later, Thomas Denny altered its course so that it flowed along the side of the mall.

Tralee Castle
The Great Castle of the Earl of Desmond
Parish: Tralee: Traighlí—strand of Lee river
Townland: Tralee: idem

This was the castle of the Earl of Desmond and for over four hundred years was the chief seat of the Desmond family. Unfortunately, nothing now remains of this famous castle, which was situated in the centre of the modern town on Denny Street. It was built some time in the thirteenth century by the Fitzgeralds (see the story of Gerald, the sixteenth Earl of Desmond, in *Old Kerry Records,*

p. 112) but there is no reliable history of the fortunes of this castle until around 1550.

It is said to have been a tower house of some considerable size, with the river Lee running around its base. By picking bits and pieces out of the various sources it can be assumed that it was a substantial tower house, if not two joined together by a lesser-sized building and surrounded by a wall and maybe having some sort of a bawn. Many restorations and changes were carried out over the centuries, including a number of additions inside the main wall, including stables, rooms and servants' quarters. It was described as a maze of chambers, rooms and saloons, which were all well appointed.

Tralee Castle was regarded as the main stronghold of the Desmonds during their uprising. In 1586, Sir Thomas Norrey advised Lord Burleigh that he would be given the possession of Tralee as part of the Desmond forfeiture. Later, when Tralee Castle was delivered to Norrey, it was in complete ruins after the rebellion, as the castle and town had been burned to the ground in 1580. The chief seat of the Earl of Desmond during this period was at Carrignafeela Castle. Later, in 1587, Sir Edward Denny, son of Sir Anthony Denny of Waltham Abbey and a member of the Privy Chamber of Henry VIII, was granted Tralee Castle, which was still in a ruinous state, together with about 6,000 acres. Edward had earlier exchanged his civil employment for a military command in Ireland and was given all the advantages of enjoying the Crown favours. He attended Lord Grey at the notorious massacre at Smerwick's Fort-del-Ore and was mentioned in dispatches for his valour in this encounter and honoured with a knighthood by Elizabeth. He was later buried at Waltham Abbey, England, in 1599 amidst much pomp and ceremony. Sir Arthur Denny, his son, died in 1619 at Carrignafeela. His son Sir Edward

Denny married Ruth Roper in 1625. She was an able woman and responsible for the rebuilding of Tralee Castle. In 1651, another woman, Lady Ellen Barry, ordered further restoration of the castle.

Burned down on many occasions during a turbulent hundred years and in ruins in 1600, the Great Castle was always repaired and rebuilt as a matter of pride.

During the siege of 1641 conducted by Pierce Ferriter and Hussey, it was occupied by the besieged English force under Sir Edward Denny. It was surrendered along with Rice's Short Castle after a long siege. At the end of the rebellion, the castle and lands were granted to Sir Edward Denny by Queen Elizabeth. Leaving his son in charge of the rebuilding of the castle, Sir Edward lived at Carrignafeela Castle. (A detailed account of the siege of Tralee in 1641 is in *Kerry Archaeological Society Magazine,* vol. III, no. 14, April 1915.)

The castle was well known for the murder of Chartres, Justice Meade, Sir Henry Danvers and all their servants, while they slept, by Sir John of Desmond and his men. At the rear of the castle there was a murdering hole, which was hidden away off the back spiral staircase, near one of the chambers. It was designed as a means of escape, as it came out through a sewer channel that led to the river. This route was used to dispose of the bodies of anyone who had met their end in the castle dungeons. The Earl of Desmond used this route to enter the castle in secret and surprised Danvers and the others.

Some time later, Sir Edward Denny, grandson of the original Edward, received a grant to rebuild the castle. He lived in the castle until his death in 1712.

By 1750, the castle was about half its original size, with new outbuildings around the bawn. The large courtyard had an arched gate to the interior on one side and another gate on the other side. The castle was finally abandoned by the

Denny family, fell into ruins, and was demolished in 1826. The material was used to build houses in the town. Denny Street was founded on the site of this ancient castle.

Notes: In 1420, it was stated that the Countess of Desmond's manor and castle were situated just south-west of the edge of the town. This could refer to Ballymullen Castle.

In a survey of 1584, a castle at Tralee is referred to as Farren McBrandon, but no further information on this name has come to light. It was possibly another name for the MacElligotts' castle. On 1 September 1599, a Spanish Armada ship was driven ashore north of Fenit harbour. When the survivors pleaded with Lady Denny to be spared, they were all hanged on the orders of Lord Denny.

Trant Castle
Parish Kildrum: Cill Dromuinn—the church on the hill
Townland: Ballymeentrant: Baile Aimin Treant
Location: the east side of Ventry harbour
O.S. map 70 ref 982 405

It has been said that Cahir Trant was the last area held by the Danes before their final defeat. However, the Trants are now generally believed to have been Normans who came over to Ireland with Strongbow.

Garret Trant was the first to advise the Earl of Clancare of the arrival of the Spanish force at Dun-an-Oir. James Trant tried to negotiate between the Lord of Desmond and Sir William Winter during the Desmond uprising but in vain.

Richard Trant was sovereign of Dingle in 1592. In 1605, Richard Rice took over the Trant castle and property. After siding with King James, the Trants lost all their property in and around Dingle and, after the death of Sir Patrick Trant, only a small section was regranted to his wife, Lady Helen.

One of the Trants of Dingle accompanied Donal Cam O'Sullivan's sons to Spain, taking a ship from Castlehaven in West Cork.

Despite the confiscations of 1584, 1641 and 1688, the Trants managed to hold on to some property around Dingle, even though many of the Trant men fought on the Continent, where they mostly lost their lives. The women of that family married into English families.

Note: For the Trant castle near Listowel, see Ballinruddery Castle.

Appendix I

Alternate Names
Ballingoleen *see* Burnham
Ballingowan *see* Ratass
Beaulieu Castle *see* Beal
Bernagrillagh *see* Ballygrellagh
Bunaneer *see* Castle Cove
Castle Connell *see* Castle Gregory
Castle Conway *see* Killorglin
Castle Moore *see* Moorestown
Castle Morris *see* Ballymullen
Castle Sybil *see* Ferriter's
D'Cantillon's *see* Rathmorrel
Dune Castle *see* Doon
Dunorlan *see* Ferriter's
Great Castle *see* Tralee
Kilmurray *see* Ballycushlane
Leap Castle *see* Ballingarry
Leck *see* Bebhion
MacAndrew *see* Tallagh
MacEllistrim *see* Tralee
Pierce *see* Ballymacaquim
Pool Castle *see* Castlelough
Ratass *see* Ballybeggan
Rice Castle *see* Tralee (Short Castle)
Shangarry *see* Kenmare
Srugreena *see* Short Castle 1
Trant Castle near Listowel *see* Ballinruddery

Bibliography

Analecta Hibernica, No. 4.
Archaeological Survey—North Kerry.
Archaeological Survey—Iveragh.
Archaeological Survey—South Kerry.
Archaeological Survey—Corca Duibne.
Kerry Archaeological Magazine.
Maps/Charts—Denny 1898. King, Brooks and O.S.
North Kerry Archaeological Magazine.
Shannonside Annuals.

Barrington, T.J., *Discovering Kerry*, Blackwater, Dublin, 1976.
Bary, V., *Houses of Kerry*, Ballinakilla Press, 1994.
Butler, W.E.T., *Gleanings from Irish History*, Longman, London, 1964.
Butler, W., *Confiscation in Irish History*.
Colman, *Castles and Abbeys of County Kerry*.
Connellan, *Annals of the Four Masters*.
Crofton Croker, T., *Legends of Kerry*.
Croker, M.B., *In the Kingdom of Kerry*, Chatto, London, 1896.
Curtis, E., *A History of Mediaeval Ireland*, Maunsel, Dublin, 1923.
Fallon, N., *The Armada in Ireland*.
Foley, P., *History of the County of Kerry—Corkaguiny*, Dublin, 1907.
Gwynne, Rev. Aubrey, *Cromwell's Policy of Transportation*.
Gaughan, J.A., *Listowel and its Vicinity*, 1973.
Hayward, R., *Munster and the City of Cork*, Phoenix House, London, 1964.
Hayward, R., *In the Kingdom of Kerry*, Dundalgan, Dundalk, 1946.

Healy, J.N., *The Castles of County Cork*, Mercier, Cork, 1988.
Hickson, M.A., *Selections from Old Kerry Records*, Watson, London, 1872.
Joyce, P.W., *Irish Names of Places*, Longman, London, 1873.
King, Jer., *County Kerry Past and Present*, Hodges Figgis, Dublin, 1931
King, J., *History of Kerry.*
Leask, H.G., *Irish Castles and Castellated Houses.*
MacCarthy, D., *Life and Letters of MacCarthy Mór*, Longman, London, 1867.
O'Brien, B., *Irish History 1691–1870*, Paul Keegan, London, 1907.
O'Brien, B., *Munster at War*, Mercier, Cork, 1971.
O'Brien, H., *The Round Towers of Ireland*, Thacker & Co., London, 1898.
O'Bryen, W., *Keating's History of Ireland.*
O'Curry, *Manuscript Materials of Irish History.*
O'Connell, D., *A Memory of Ireland Native and Saxon*, Dolman, Dublin, 1849.
O'Donovan, J., (ed.) *Miscellany of the Celtic Society*, Dublin, 1849.
O'Donovan, J., *The Antiquities of the County of Kerry*, 1841.
O'Grady, S., (ed.) *Pacata Hibernia*, Downey, London, 1896.
O'Sullivan, Don P., *Ireland under Elizabeth.*
Smith, C., *The Ancient and Present State of the County of Kerry*, Guys, Cork.
Taylor & Skinner, *Maps of the Roads of Ireland*, London.
Windele, J., *South of Ireland*, Bradford & Co., Cork, 1849.
Windele, J., *Killarney*, Bradford & Co., Cork, 1849.